GRANDPARENTS
ENJOYING AND CARING FOR YOUR GRANDCHILD

GRANDPARENTS
ENJOYING AND CARING FOR YOUR GRANDCHILD

Dr. Miriam Stoppard

LONDON, NEW YORK, MUNICH,
MELBOURNE, AND DELHI

*For my 11 grandchildren who, each in their own
way, have given me untold pleasure and love.*

DK India
Senior Editor Pakshalika Jayaprakash
Designers Ira Sharma, Mini Dhawan, Balwant Singh
Managing Editor Suchismita Banerjee
Managing Art Editor Romi Chakraborty
DTP Designer Manish Chandra Upreti
DTP Manager Sunil Sharma
Picture Researcher Sakshi Saluja

DK US and UK
US Editors Jane Perlmutter and Shannon Beatty
Project Editor Daniel Mills
Senior Art Editor Isabel de Cordova
Managing Editor Penny Warren
Managing Art Editors Glenda Fisher
    and Marianne Markham
Publisher Peggy Vance
Art Directors Peter Luff and Lisa Lanzarini
Production Editor Ben Marcus
Creative Technical Support Sonia Charbonnier
Senior Production Controller Man Fai Lau

Edited for DK by Jinny Johnson
Photography by Ruth Jenkinson

First American Edition, 2011

Published in the United States by
DK Publishing
375 Hudson Street
New York, New York 10014

11 12 13 14 15   10 9 8 7 6 5 4 3 2 1
001–175302–Aug/2011

Copyright © 2011 Dorling Kindersley Limited
Text copyright © 2011 Miriam Stoppard
All rights reserved

Published in Great Britain by Dorling Kindersley Limited.

ISBN 978-0-7566-8223-1

DK books are available at special discounts when
purchased in bulk for sales promotions, premiums,
fund-raising, or educational use. For details, contact: DK
Publishing Special Markets, 375 Hudson Street, New York,
New York 10014 or SpecialSales@dk.com.

Printed and bound in Singapore by Tien Wah Press

Discover more at
www.dk.com

Contents

8 *Good times with Grandma and Grandpa* — 160

5 *Comforting your grandchild* — 98

6 *Sweet dreams with Grandma and Grandpa* — 114

9 *Grandparent as caregiver* — 182

10 *First aid* — 196

7 *Learning and play* — 138

Introduction

I've written this book for today's grandparents, who are different than those of any other generation. We belong to the 21st century and we're engaged with life as it is lived today, be it travel, the internet, or new technology. This kind of grandparent is not an observer but part of the mainstream and wants to be up to date with everything that's going on. We are active, informed, and involved, and the same is true when it comes to child care.

It's the nature of today's Grandma and Grandpa to be curious about how child-care advice has changed since they were bringing up their own children. They want to be well informed, so they can understand and appreciate the routines and techniques that their children and children-in-law (from now on called son and daughter, whether in-law or not) practice.

Being informed in this way will act as good preparation for being a formal or informal caregiver of grandchildren, and it'll give you the confidence to act alone if that's what's called for. It will also mean that conflict is avoided when you find your old methods at odds with those of your children, because you will understand the reasoning behind new child-care techniques.

"Today's grandparents want to be well informed, so they can understand and appreciate the child-care techniques that their children practice"

I have to confess another goal in writing this book—it's so that you'll be armed with knowledge that will make you prepared to stand back and generously admit that your children have the right to bring up their children the way that they want to, even if you think the way they're going about it is wrong. My mother tried to interfere with the way I brought up my children, and I vowed I wouldn't repeat that with my grandchildren. I'm not saying it will always be easy. It won't. But you have decades of experience that have taught you forbearance and tolerance. Your children need those qualities just as much as they need your wisdom and experience.

Of course there will be lots of situations where your own tried-and-tested baby- and child-care methods are as useful as ever, and even if you feel a bit rusty at first, you'll soon recall how you used to manage things. It'll all come flooding back to you in an instant.

Nonetheless there will be a lot of new stuff to get familiar with. Today's parents do quite a few important things differently than us. How and when to start solid food has moved a long way since we were introducing solids to our babies. Self-introduction of solids is a new and useful concept, which I advocate. You'll also find that parents have new approaches to sleeping and crying and I'd advise you to bone up on terms like "rapid return" and "controlled crying," which are explained for you in this book.

Then there's the concept of a time out, something I've witnessed in action many times and which works wonderfully well. I often wished I'd known about it for my own children. You'll find potty training has been largely abandoned, thank heavens, and children's socializing has greatly increased with play dates and sleepovers.

You may find yourself in a family situation where your contribution to child care is really useful. It may even be essential, for example if your help allows your son and daughter to work to swell the household purse. I sometimes get letters from grandparents who feel their contribution to child care goes unacknowledged and unappreciated. Don't let yourself fall into this trap. If you're going to be taking care of your grandchild on a regular basis, try to reach an agreement with your son and daughter about the things you are and aren't prepared to do, and about how much time you can give. You may want to consider negotiating payment for your duties, especially if you are taking the place of a nanny or preschool—if so, make sure you bring this subject up in your initial discussions so resentment won't fester.

A special connection
There is no substitute for the one-on-one special attention that you can give your grandchildren. You are their ideal caregiver, playmate, and teacher.

I've written this book with the goal of increasing your comfort level through any new situation you may find yourself in as a grandparent, including broader issues such as being Grandma and Grandpa to step-grandchildren, dealing with other grandparents, and staying in touch with family at a distance.

Grandchildren are a blessing which can take us by surprise as we get older. They're certainly one of the things that make getting older an unexpected delight. I'd like to think this book will only increase your joy in your new family members, and introduce you to new pleasures.

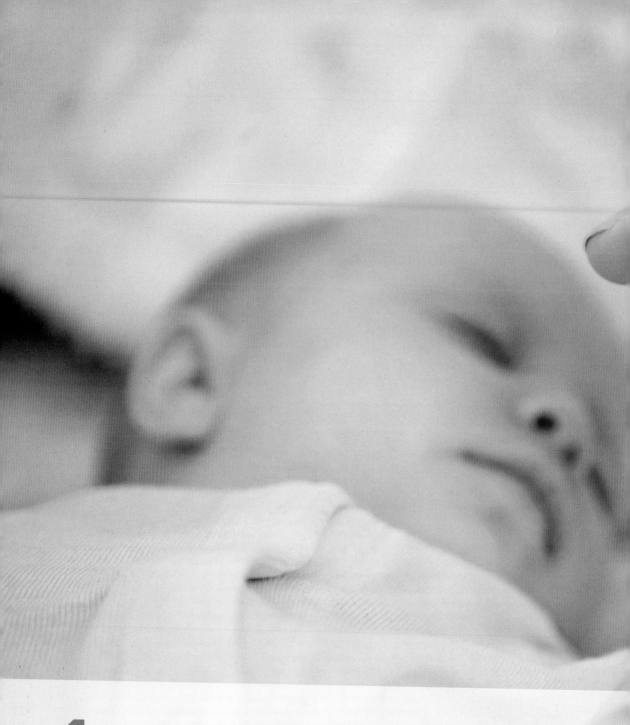

1 Being a Grandparent

You'll fall head-over-heels in love with your new grandchild. And you'll discover that your relationship with him is all-important.

You are a grandparent

With the birth of my first grandchild I discovered a new me. I didn't know I had this grandmother inside me. I didn't know I would feel like this and how thrilled I would be. I fell head-over-heels in love with my grandchildren and I've been rewarded with really special relationships.

Your real usefulness

I always suspected there was a good reason why women live so long after menopause and the end of their fertile lives, so I was fascinated to read a study on female longevity, published in 2004. The authors looked at communities in 18th- and 19th-century Finland and Canada and discovered that women gained two extra grandchildren for every decade they lived beyond the age of 50.

Furthermore, women whose mothers were alive had more babies and at a younger age, and the births were closer together. This goes a long way to supporting my conviction that women are programmed to live beyond menopause to help our children with their children. The same happens in many other animal societies. An elephant family, for example, is led by an older female—a grandmother—on whose wisdom the whole herd depends.

"Grandparents are more important now than ever and provide much needed support. In the US, a majority of children receive some care from grandparents"

Why grandparents are important

Life in the 21st century is very different to the way those communities lived, but grandparents are more important than ever. At a time when most families need two salaries in order to make ends meet, grandparents provide much needed childcare support. In the US a majority of children receive some care from their grandparents. And by virtue of their age and experience, grandparents can generally be more patient, philosophical, and sympathetic than other caregivers. A grandparent can relieve busy parents and so help support the whole family.

How you feel about being a grandparent

Most mothers and fathers welcome the transition to grandparenthood. Most women long to be a grandma and are thrilled when their first grandchild arrives. But this reaction isn't universal. I've had letters from women who feel it comes too soon, and makes it seem they're getting old before their time.

There's pleasure to be had from grandchildren that is unique and, in some ways, greater than the love of parents for their children. It's certainly different and, if you're lucky, it isn't interrupted by chores or diluted by cares and worries.

"By virtue of their age and experience, grandparents can generally be more patient, philosophical, and sympathetic than other caregivers"

I have found that this very special kind of love can be given free rein because there's room for patience, for undivided attention, for focus on my grandchild's needs, and for unconditional love. I can indulge all these feelings because I now have the time and the space in my life.

For me the greatest surprise was how I rediscovered, through my grandchildren, the love I had felt for my own sons when they were babies. This is something we believe has been left behind. But there, with your first grandchild, you experience again the love you thought would never return.

What will you be called?

Each family will come up with their own favorite names for grandparents that everyone likes and feels comfortable with. Your preference should be in the mix and you can influence the outcome by using your favorite name yourself. I always saw myself as Granny, and I found myself saying to everyone "Oh, Granny can do that," rather than using "I."

Of course, there may be a family tradition for grandparents to be called Grandma and Grandpa, and Grandad is an option for grandfathers. Then again, there's Nana for grandmothers.

In families when there is more than one set of grandparents first names are needed to make distinctions. So in two of my children's families, I'm known as Granny Miri.

What about grandpas?

I'm a great fan of grandpas and so are grandchildren. From an early age babies and children of both genders have a soft spot for the men in the family. It strikes me that this is because, in every family, there's no shortage of women cooing over and taking care of the babies and children. But now and then babies enjoy the lower tones of men's voices, the large, firm, masculine hands, and the reassuring smell of male skin.

As children get older their relationship with Grandpa can become very close and loving. By and large, grandpas are gentle, quiet, and playful—qualities all children warm to. Most grandpas are only too happy to tell their grandchildren stories about when they were young. Grandchildren find this irresistible and will ask for more and more stories. Grandparents generally have more time than dads for rough and tumble games, and if Grandpa's healthy enough to get down on the floor he'll be a grandchild's favorite.

How can I best help?

There are many different ways of being a grandparent. You may be lucky enough to live nearby and have time to babysit and be an extra pair of hands at the drop of a hat. But if you live a far away, even in another country, technology can help you be a familiar presence to your grandchildren as you chat on the computer and send regular emails.

A helping hand

You might think that a busy new mom welcomes help in any form, and she does, but never forget that you are doing just that—helping. You are not in charge and you must do what you are told. Otherwise your offers may become much less welcome. If you get it right, there are many ways you can lend a hand, depending on your circumstances.

In some families, grandparents take a very active part in child care while parents work. For single-parent families, grandparent care may be the only way the parent can manage to work outside the home. If grandparents are still working themselves or have other commitments, help may take the form of a regular babysitting slot so parents can take a much-needed night out together, or an outing with grandchildren on the weekend.

> **" *Never forget that you are helping—you are not in charge and you must do what you are told* "**

Long-distance grandparenting has been revolutionized by the internet, which allows you not only to talk with your grandchildren without worrying about the phone bill, but also to see each other, via the computer camera, as you talk. And of course you can send e-mails as they get older.

How much do you want to do?

Some grandparents, particularly grandmas, find it difficult to deal with their irresistible desire to help with newborn and young grandchildren. It's easy to want to be involved more than is good for you, and to commit to doing more than you can manage. My advice is to go carefully at first. Offer to help but never—ever—try to take over.

Some things are more exhausting than others. Helping with meals and bath times, reading books at bedtime, picking up grandchildren from school are all tasks that are pleasurable and not too taxing. But to take on full-time child care for even one grandchild so that your daughter or daughter-in-law can work, for instance, can be exhausting, depending on your age. Doing night duty for babies or young children, for example, could quickly wear you out.

The fatigue is a lot to deal with and you have to decide if this is how you saw this stage of your life. Just as important, is this how your partner saw it. Will he mind you being absent for long stretches of time when he may have been expecting to spend newly found, cherished "us-time" with you?

Making it clear what you can and can't do

It may not be easy to be forthright with your children when you feel pulled in two directions. Your loyalty to them and your grandchildren may feel painfully stretched since you want to help but also want to make time for yourself and your partner. But it's a conversation you have to broach. Without it, you may find your resentment building, especially if your help is taken for granted and goes unacknowledged. If you're going to get deeply involved in child care, there's also the question of payment, and while most grandparents don't want to take money, it's a subject worth raising if you provide significant child care.

Your priorities

It's only fair to your children that you make your priorities clear so that their expectations fit yours. Different expectations can result in strife. It may be that you prefer set times when you help out—for example, Wednesday afternoons and

Learning together
Take every opportunity to be with your grandchildren and expand their knowledge of the world. Play with them together and the younger will start to learn from the older.

Friday mornings, as well as ad hoc babysitting duties. Or you may feel more comfortable with a casual arrangement, with you being an extra pair of hands occasionally or having a grandchild for a sleepover once in a while. For you to get the most out of grandparenting your involvement has to mesh with your children's needs—and your own.

"Resist the temptation to take sides and strive to be a grandparent who's nice to know—one who is helpful, cheerful, and makes light of minor problems"

Wise grandmas

As a grandmother to 11 grandchildren I've found myself adhering to certain ways of handling things that seem to work. The following is my advice for happy grandparents and families.

Respect your children's space and only visit by invitation or mutual arrangement. You'll keep communication open if you always respect your children's choices and boundaries with good intentions. Look for opportunities to praise your children on being good parents, and never undermine your children or your grandchildren. Offer support and advice without always expecting it to be accepted and keep a well-developed sense of fairness and humor. Resist the temptation to take sides and try to be a grandparent who's nice to know—one who is helpful, cheerful, and makes light of minor problems.

I'm not suggesting all this is easy. It's not. You may have to change the way you think and behave about some things. And you may have to make many concessions and sacrifices, but it'll be worth it in my experience. Being a grandparent is an opportunity to grow and that's an offer we can't refuse.

Ways of helping
Perhaps you can take your grandson to preschool some days, bringing the younger one along to give Mom a break? Or your could invite your grandchild to your house for a sleepover.

Watch and listen

Always remember that your grandchildren are your children's children—not yours—and be careful to respect that. It's your children who set the house rules, and if you flout those or disagree, you're asking for trouble. As a grandparent, you are a team member, not a team leader.

Changing attitudes

If you believe that you know best about bringing up your grandchildren, think again. It's 20 or 30 years, maybe more, since you had your own children, and things have moved on a great deal. Your children are following modern child-care guidelines on such matters as feeding and sleep patterns, and your old rules of thumb no longer apply.

Certainly there is an aspect of fashion about child-care methods—some things go in and out of fashion—but other changes, such as the safest way to put babies down to sleep in their cribs (see page 120) to reduce the risk of crib death (SIDS), are based on good, solid research.

Never assume that the old ways are best—they're not always, and you will only aggravate your children if you try to insist on following outdated methods. Be open to the latest ideas and you may be surprised at how good they are. There's new advice for preparing bottles of formula (see page 55), which is very sensible; diapers, strollers, and lots more have changed. It's a different world, so be ready to learn from your children and adapt willingly to their methods.

"Never assume that the old ways are best—they're not always and you will only aggravate your children if you try to insist on following outdated methods"

Your supporting role

Older generations of women have always felt they had the right to interfere in child care, but not any more. I'm sure there were times when you resented your parents' interference while you were bringing up your children. I know I did. I imagine you wished they'd mind their own business, especially if your views were dramatically opposed.

So forget the idea that you are older and wiser, and therefore can impose your will on a younger, less experienced generation. It could be that you're way out of date. Better to bone up on the latest theories so that you can trade ideas as equals. You'll be a better grandparent for it. Of course, there are times when I think my children might do the occasional thing differently, but I've learned to hold my tongue. And time and time again, I've realized that their new ways are better than mine. Granny doesn't always know best.

I believe it's asking for trouble if you flout your children's wishes when they're not present, thinking that you do know best and hoping they won't find out. But you will be found out and you may find yourself on the wrong end of an argument with your children, from which you can't escape. Concentrate on the positives and ignore the negatives. It's neither useful nor productive to do otherwise. It's the same with your children's parenting skills. Your only role is to support.

Defer to the parents

Follow the rules
Do your best to adhere to the house rules when you're at your daughter's home. If you remember that she's in charge, you'll always be a very welcome visitor.

I've found a good habit to cultivate is to defer to your children about anything when you're in doubt, or just as a courtesy. When your grandchild asks your permission for something—another cookie, or to get out the paints, paper, and smock and do some painting—it's so easy to say, "If Mommy (or Daddy) thinks it's OK, that's fine." It's also reassuring for your children and gratifying for your grandchildren to hear you say, "Wasn't that smart of Daddy," or "Good job, Mommy." It's a real bonding mannerism to cultivate and helps build trust between you and your children all the time.

If something happens that has the potential to be really divisive and possibly ruin your relationship forever, instead of taking up the moral high ground you can decide to support your child through thick and thin. That way, if things ever get really bad, they will turn to you. You're there to pick up the pieces; you aren't there to smash china. If you're big enough to do that, your children will be grateful and loving for as long as you live.

Different ways of bringing up children

There are fashions and fads in how parents tackle their role and they come and go. My mother was brought up according to the discipline of "spare the rod and spoil the child." I myself was brought up to believe that my parents' word was law and not to be questioned, and you may have been too. Today's parenting style is quite different, and in my belief, it's better than mine was. Today's parents are child-oriented in a way previous generations of parents never were.

Fun with cooking
Children love cooking with Grandma. It's never too early to start teaching your grandchild about preparing food, particularly something like baking, which is fun and very safe.

Modern parents are careful not to raise their voices, not to frown in disapproval, not to make a fuss over small things, and to make light of mistakes and accidents. They don't sweat the small stuff and carefully choose which battles to fight. They enjoy their role as teacher, whether it's getting down on the carpet to do a jigsaw puzzle, pointing out why trees lose their leaves in the fall, or making space for a three-year-old to help with the cooking.

I find the present-day approach to discipline very attractive—a child is given a clear chance and lots of space to choose to do as they've been told and correct bad behavior. It's a kind and humanitarian approach to say:

"I'm going to ask you again to put away your toys."
"This is the third time I'm asking and I won't ask again, you'll get a time out."
"I'm going to count to five then give you a time out."
Then, either
"Well done and thank you for picking up your toys."
Or
"Time out." (for as many minutes as his or her age)
The time-out routine is completed in a wholly sensible way so that a child learns a new lesson in behaving. It goes like this:
"Do you know why you were in a time out?"
"Yes, because I wouldn't pick up my toys."
"Yes, and because you didn't do what Mommy asked. Are you going to say sorry?"
"Sorry Mommy."
"Good boy." (big hug) "Mommy loves you. Now let's have a snack."

It's clear from this re-enactment that an authoritarian parenting style is not in fashion. Today's parents prefer negotiation to laying down the law. Uppermost in their minds is to achieve a sensible, firm resolution to problems without resorting to punishments—and certainly no yelling and spanking—while still clearly defining boundaries.

Many good things result from this approach. A child feels like a valued member of the family, one with a voice and with choices and who is shown respect. This environment encourages self-discipline, self-esteem, thoughtfulness for others, and a sense of responsibility.

There will be grandparents who feel this is too lax an approach to child rearing, but it's important to resist the temptation to interfere. There's no more dangerous minefield than differing views on discipline.

In my way of thinking it's even more important to remain silent if you feel parents are being too tough. It wouldn't be in your grandchild's interests for you to fall out with his parents and be banned from the house. Then you wouldn't be around to ameliorate the situation and comfort your grandson or granddaughter.

Of course, if your grandchild's in any kind of danger from poor parenting it's your job to put the interests of the child before those of his parents. But it's vital to be absolutely sure of your position before leaping in. Think very carefully and even collect evidence before creating a potentially incendiary situation that will not serve your grandchild.

Talking to your grandchild

Victorian nannies had the right idea—they started to talk when their charges woke up and never stopped until they fell asleep. Today's adults should do the same, even when a baby is small, when the baby can't say a word, and we think the baby doesn't understand anything we're saying. A baby may not comprehend individual words, but he does gradually grasp the sense. And he learns the rhythm of conversation, and gets the hang of question-and-answer and the rise and fall of speech.

Babies who are spoken and sung to a lot, and who listen to nursery rhymes and clapping games, speak early. If you're the person doing the speaking and the singing, you start a dialogue with your grandchild that continues as long as you live. Of course there are a few tricks. Making eye contact helps your grandchild learn and respond. Swinging around to face him when he asks a question gives him confidence.

When your grandchild is very young, saying anything is more important than what you say, and an early conversation with your baby grandchild in a singsong voice will slowly graduate to quite grown-up exchanges. From the age of three, when your grandchild begins to express fairly complex concepts, I believe in using adult words to enlarge his vocabulary while, for example, describing how something works. You can add a simple explanation in parenthesis. And once they reach five, I often say, "Here's a great new word for you," and I explain its use.

New relationships

The advent of a new baby can bring family dynamics into full focus. Whereas your son was simply your son and your daughter-in-law was simply your daughter-in-law, relationships now become more important and different. Your son becomes the father of your grandchild, and your daughter-in-law her mother. That changes them and your relationship to them. This change in relationships extends right across the family (or families), creating the need for reappraisal and adjustment, which isn't always without tension and uncertainty. But getting along has to be the highest priority, not seniority.

The other grandparents

Before the arrival of your grandchild you enjoyed a one-to-one relationship with your son (in law) and daughter (in law), but now you may be one of possibly several grandparents, depending on how extended the family is. I have four sons, four daughters-in-law, and two stepdaughters with families of their own in which there are second marriages. The result is that I am only one of four grandmothers in these particular families. Furthermore I'm pretty low in the hierarchy—fourth in fact. Being fourth taught me a lot about restraint, tolerance, flexibility, and gratitude (for being included as a grandmother at all), and I've taken these qualities to my closer family.

> **" *Grandchildren change the relationships within a family, creating the need for reappraisal and adjustment* "**

Even here the relationships weren't straightforward. The parents of one of my daughters-in-law live in overseas, and so they see much less of her and our grandchildren than I do. When they visit, they have first dibs on seeing the grandchildren and I gladly give them space. For their part, they exhibit not the slightest rivalry with me—which they easily could. Their relationship with me is motivated by appreciation of what I do for their daughter, her family, and her children. They are an object lesson to me and all grandparents.

Unfortunately, things aren't always so easy, and rivalry between grandparents is quite common. In my experience, though, behaving generously always pays off and makes for good family relationships.

Avoiding rivalries

It's just as well grandparenthood comes when we've had time to figure out how to deal with difficult emotions like jealousy and insecurity. By the time we become grandparents we've learned the value of generosity, understanding, even sacrifice, and you may be called upon to exercise all of these qualities. It will probably come easier to you now than at any time previously because you're clear what your goals are: continuing to see your grandchild, and keeping the channels of communication open and relationships generally sweet.

Dealing with cultural differences

Religion is the toughest one, but even that must be dealt with calmly and sympathetically. You may have to summon up all your Solomon-like wisdom.

I was raised an Orthodox Jew and I am an atheist. One of my daughters-in-law recently embraced Catholicism and wanted to baptize her children into her faith. The christening was a big family affair. Would I exclude myself on the grounds of our differing beliefs? No way. My overriding concern was for my daughter-in-law to celebrate her faith and enjoy the occasion. I wouldn't have wanted to spoil the day in any way and create no-go areas for the future. With these priorities in mind, any cultural differences can be negotiated.

" *If you do encounter family rivalries, remember that your grandchild is equally important to you all, and her welfare comes first* **"**

You and your daughter / son

I'm sure when you were bringing up your children you wanted to raise them your way and resented interference from mothers and mothers-in-law. It's worth remembering this when it comes to your son's or daughter's own parenting style. Their preferences must rule, and we have only one role—to bow to them.

In fact there are pleasant surprises if you stand back and give your children space to be the parents they want to be. You'll watch them becoming better parents than you were. You'll see them using parenting strategies that will make you start nodding in approval. And it can give all grandmas great pleasure to be able to say, "How well you deal with that," or, "I wish I'd known to do that." It will feel quite natural to defer to your children and ask them how you can help. Be proud of your son or daughter and tell them so.

You and your daughter- or son-in-law

With these family members you only share a short common history. Sons- and daughters-in-law have rafts of experience that are unknown to you. They're closer to their friends and their own family than they are to you, and all these relationships and loyalties must be respected.

Because your common ground hasn't been established through childhood to adulthood it would be a foolhardy grandparent who rushed in and started throwing her weight around. Just think back for a moment to when you were a young parent and your mother-in-law tried to tell you how to take care of your baby. I remember those times and how upset I felt. I just wanted to tell her to butt out and leave me alone. You may have similar memories, so be careful not to make the same mistakes.

It's worth remembering that a son- or daughter-in-law is bound to be more nervous and insecure about you and how you might judge them as parents than your own son or daughter. Even chance negative remarks can assume great meaning and raise hackles. So my two golden rules are praise where you can (and there's always something worth praising) and bite your tongue before criticizing. If you follow these rules, you'll find you're always welcomed by your daughter- or son-in-law.

Focus on your grandchild
Your grandchild loves everyone in her family so you need never feel you have to compete for her attention. Focus on your grandchild and you will all enjoy having fun together.

"Ask what you can do to help and support the family. And remember—you're a team member, not a team leader"

"I disagree with my daughter-in-law"

Annie has problems with her daughter-in-law. In fact, she's disliked her from the start and can't think why her son ever married her. Now there are two children—a girl of three-and-a-half and a boy of eight months—and Annie is seriously worried. The house is always a mess and her daughter-in-law is disorganized and doesn't seem to discipline the children. Annie thinks that her grandchildren are going to suffer if their mom doesn't mend her ways. What can she do?

each have our own way of doing things, and even if Annie strongly disagrees with their lifestyle and the way they're bringing up their children, that doesn't make her right and her son and daughter-in-law wrong.

As a grandparent, you're called upon to have the wisdom of Solomon and the patience of Job. You may sometimes have to step over the mess to get into the house, and find it hard to make space on the kitchen table to put down the fruit you've brought them. Remember you're a visitor. This isn't your home. You have no rights

I suggest Annie tries to look at things in a more positive light and see if she can help the family out, rather than criticize

Not a lot. Annie's daughter-in-law clearly doesn't care about keeping a neat house or being strict with her children. If Annie confronts her head-on about her worries she risks an all-out argument and losing touch with her grandchildren.

Perhaps it is better to live and let live. If Annie's daughter-in-law, and incidentally her son, want to live in a perpetual mess that's their choice. And if they don't take a firm hand with their children—Annie's grandchildren—that's their prerogative. We

here, nor do you have jurisdiction over how your grandchildren are brought up.

I feel that Annie is biased against her daughter-in-law—she says she has disliked her from the start—and I would suggest she gives her a break. Instead of resenting her daughter-in-law, I would suggest Annie tries to look at things in a more positive light and see if she can help the family out, rather than criticize. And she might thank her lucky stars she's welcome to visit. A lot of grandparents aren't.

2 *Your New Grandchild*

Do all you can to support the new family in these early weeks, but tread carefully at first, and remember that you're not in charge.

Birth now

Childbirth has changed a lot since we were having babies. Gone are the days when a woman had to lie on her back with her legs in the air to give birth. Gone, too, are enemas, the shaving of pubic hair, and lack of choices. Instead we have birthing pools, ambulant epidurals, doulas, hypnobirthing, and midwives. Labor and birth are a lot less prescribed now than they used to be, and Mom is in charge.

How moms prepare for the birth now

Prenatal classes, particularly during the last couple of months, concentrate on couples rather than just the mom-to-be. Husbands and fathers are much more involved than they used to be, and they are actively encouraged to be at the birth, help complete a birth plan (of how the couple would like the birth to proceed, with preferences clearly emphasized), and to take a precise role at the birth and in the birthing room.

Besides the breathing techniques we all know, women are encouraged to manage their own births with the help of a doctor or midwife, the goal being for a woman to have the birth she wants and, if at all possible, to enjoy it. One of the more rare recent advances in childbirth is hypnobirthing. During five

"While still rare, the number of midwife-attended deliveries is increasing—something I heartily approve of"

prenatal sessions a woman can be prepared for the birth by learning from a hypnotherapist how to enter a natural state of profound relaxation. She can visualize a safe, normal, natural, and comfortable birth, which brings a sense of control. By imagining the birth going smoothly, fear is eliminated. Similarly, visualizing successful breast-feeding encourages a woman to act intuitively and put her baby to her breast as soon as she holds him.

A more natural birth

While a vast majority of pregnant women are cared for by obstetricians, the number of midwife-attended deliveries is increasing—something I heartily approve of. Many women now do try to have more natural deliveries. Birthing centers staffed by midwives are available and focus on more natural deliveries (some are free-standing and some are affiliated with hospitals in case medical intervention is needed). Some centers have birthing pools available if a woman wants to immerse herself to rest between contractions and relieve pain. Midwives may be able to arrange for birthing pools at home.

" *Labor and birth are a lot less prescribed now than they used to be, and Mom is in charge* "

Birth preferences

Expectant mothers these days play a much more active role than ever in voicing their preferences about how they hope labor and delivery will take place, and that sometimes includes the choice of whether to have a midwife or an obstetrician attend the birth and whether to deliver at a conventional hosipital or a birthing center. For many mothers, the ultimate perference is to have natural birth. Certainly a holistic approach has become much more popular. Birthing Centers can offer the familiar surroundings of home. With her family around her, a woman can feel relaxed, in command of the situation, and secure; these are all factors that can help a birth to go smoothly, quickly, and less painfully.

Midwives lead the way

Midwives are starting to assume the central role I've always thought they should have. When midwives are in charge, there are fewer interventions (such as cesarean or the use of forceps) and the requests of the mother are paramount. These days, mothers who can afford it may like a doula to be present too. A doula is a birthing expert (but not necessarily a qualified midwife), who is there solely to look after the birthing woman's needs and to give support, not only to the mother but also to the couple. Doulas can help birthing women in many

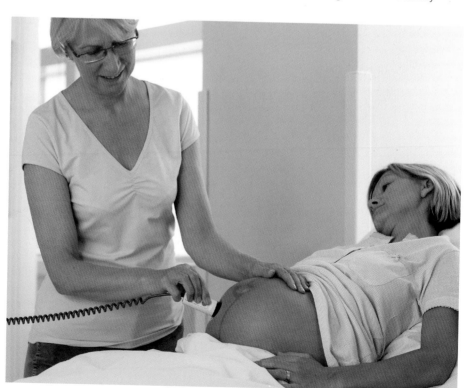

Routine scans
Ultrasounds are routine at 8–12 weeks and at 18–22 weeks to check on the progress of the baby. Ask your daughter to bring you a picture so you can have your first look of your grandchild.

ways, by giving encouragement, massage, help with breathing, and guidance on what to expect. They can also give treatments such as aromatherapy as well as psychological support before, during, and after the birth. In fact, doulas can do anything that a woman or couple asks for, in the way they want.

If you're having a less interventionist, midwife-attended birth you might find the midwife is doing less than what was done in your day—there are fewer internal examinations and, as the baby is being born, she hovers, waiting rather than helping the baby out. This is the HOOP technique (Hands Off Or Poised) and is still a bit rare and somewhat difficult to find in the US but has just as successful birthing results as the older, hands-on technique.

> " *Today's moms are outspoken and active participants. They call the shots and they want to* "

The rise and rise of cesarean sections

Cesarean sections are much more common than they used to be. In my time a cesarean was confined to medical necessity and I believe it still should be. But now cesareans may be given for a number of reasons such as controlling the date and time of the birth, fear of labor pain, anxiety over pelvic floor laxity and incontinence after the birth, and so on. None of these is justification enough for a cesarean. Nonetheless, the latest figures suggest that about one in three babies born in the US is delivered surgically, and if your daughter opts for that your job is to support her.

Mother-to-be is queen

I think you'll notice that pregnancy, labor, and birth now are mother-centric: everything centers on the mother, her preferences, her needs, and her comfort. Everyone in there is working to make sure she gets the birth she desires. And rightly so. Today's moms-to-be are outspoken and active participants. They call the shots and they want to. They question the customary practices and, with the help of the internet, explore all the options surrounding childbirth.

When I first wrote about choices in childbirth, the idea that women could choose was considered new-fangled and against the "natural order" of things (imposed by doctors). These days, I'm very glad to see that women are in position to choose.

How can I help in the beginning?

The guiding principle here is not what you would like to do but what your children would like you to do. Help that isn't wanted is help wasted. Worse, it may be seen as interference. When one of my daughters-in-law was expecting, I imagined being her birth coach. But when I asked her how she saw the birth she said one of her girlfriends would be with her. I remember the pang of disappointment. I had been in my own private fantasy, not thinking about her wishes at all. I remember being thankful I didn't ask directly to be her birth coach because all she could have done was to say no and that would have been painful and embarrassing for her. The same applies to baby care.

What can I do?

I'd advise any grandma of a newborn baby to ask what kind of help, if any, your children would like. If your daughter is caring for the baby around-the-clock by herself, your help could be greatly appreciated. And not only in the form of covering the occasional night, feeding, bathing, dressing, and so on. Just as helpful would be doing jobs to keep the household running. So cooking, laundry, shopping, and taking the baby out for short periods so that the new mom and dad can rest are all likely to be welcomed. In fact, the most valuable role you can take on is that of mother's help. To think of yourself in that way automatically precludes being interfering and heavy-handed. And to be included in any way in the care of a new grandchild is, in my mind, a great blessing.

"The most valuable role for you is that of mother's help. To think of yourself in that way automatically precludes your being interfering and heavy-handed"

If the parents can afford to hire a baby nurse (or you can afford to hire one for them) there may be much less for you to do. The presence of a baby nurse will mean that the baby is well taken care of and Mom and Dad will get enough rest. So the help required may amount to little more than covering for the nurse on her day off. Even so, I'm sure everyone would welcome some babysitting so that the nurse can take a nap. Taking the baby for a walk could also be useful to everyone and gives you time on your own with your new grandchild. You'll have the chance to talk endlessly, sing songs, cuddle, and let the baby get used to your smell and to the sound of your voice.

You can be especially valuable to brothers and sisters of the new baby. Making them feel loved and secure, despite Mom and Dad giving the baby most of their attention, is a vital job for you.

What can I bring?

You'll find yourself longing to rush to the store and buy anything and everything for your precious new grandchild, and that's wonderful. But think carefully before you do and find out as much as you can about your children's wants and needs. For instance, if your children are firmly on the side of eco-friendly reusable diapers, they won't welcome a truck load of disposable diapers arriving at their door.

I was taken aback at first when I asked my nephew and his wife what gift they would like for their soon-to-arrive baby and they replied, "A doula." I would never have thought of this and my gift was a huge success.

Here are a few ideas for first gifts. I suggest waiting until Mom and baby are home rather than loading them up with stuff at the hospital. There's plenty of time for the more long-lasting presents, such as children's china, cutlery, and keepsakes. At first, think practical and remember that the best gift of all is time.

- Baby basics—onesies and undershirts in larger sizes as well as newborn sizes are always welcome
- A soft shawl for wrapping and swaddling baby
- A first toy—perhaps a mobile to go over the crib
- A supply of disposable or reusable diapers—check first what's wanted
- Something for Mom, such as luxury bath oil and a promise to watch the baby while Mom takes a long soak
- Food for the freezer
- A gift certificate for a really good take-out meal for Mom and Dad, delivered to the door
- A gift certificate for cleaning help by a professional or you.

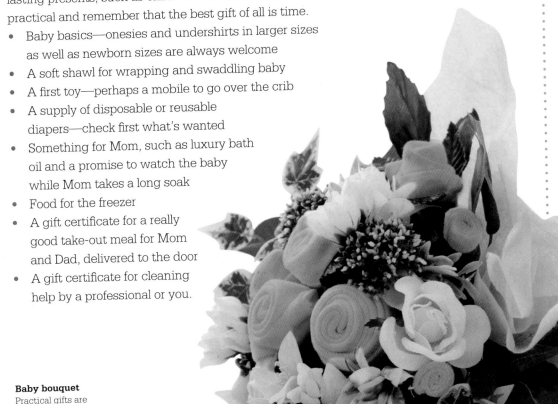

Baby bouquet
Practical gifts are always welcome but are made even more special if presented beautifully. This bouquet includes little baby clothes tucked in among the flowers.

"One important role when going to stay is helping to keep older siblings occupied while Mom and Dad get to know their new baby"

Going to stay

A wise grandma stops and considers all the implications of offering to stay before she actually agrees to do so. You should only offer if you are sure the parents will welcome you and you won't be intruding, especially in the early days. The following are some of the things to think about.

- Do you have the stamina to be on your feet for much of the day?
- Can you function properly on little sleep?
- Is your partner OK to get by without you?
- Would your own domestic arrangements suffer in your absence?
- Can you make sure you get enough breaks and rest?

The best arrangement may be to stay for a few days at a time, then take a break of a day or so to rest up, do your shopping, and see your partner. It's easy to get carried away by the love you feel for your grandchild and not want to leave her for any length of time, but it's crucial to conserve your energies if you want to be there for the long haul.

And while you're ensconced in your children's house, see to your own creature comforts while fitting in existing routines. Take your own toiletries as well as a change of clothes, comfortable sleepwear, outdoor shoes, and slippers. If at all possible, get a comfortable bed—you may not be very comfortable if you try to make do with a cot or a mattress on the floor.

" *Watch and listen to familiarize yourself with the baby's routines and the equipment the parents have opted for* "

While you have the chance, watch and listen carefully to familiarize yourself with the baby's routines and the equipment the parents have opted for. I remember having to learn how to use the chosen sterilizing equipment—I needed to watch my daughter-in-law assemble, stack, and clean it several times before I dared venture using it. It was the same with the brand of disposable diapers my children opted to use for my granddaughter. It took me quite a few tries to get them on properly, and again I learned just by standing and looking.

Another thing I needed was detailed instructions for was the baby sling. I managed to get it on but found it very difficult to take off at first. Now I am adept at this and can get the sling on and off with one hand.

Babymoon

This word derives from honeymoon—the time when two newlyweds spend quality time alone together, growing accustomed to each other in their new roles and forming a bond that can last a lifetime.

A new family
This is such an exciting time for new parents so if they want to be left alone to have a babymoon, leave them to it and don't be offended. You'll soon have plenty of time with your grandchild.

Babymoon describes exactly the same process with the inclusion of the new baby. When one of my sons first described wanting to be left alone with his wife and new baby for a week or so, with no visitors, I did feel a slight pang at being excluded. But after a moment's thought, I was convinced of their wisdom. There's no better way for new parents to bond with their newborn baby than to hole up together, shut out the world, and concentrate on each other. At the end of the week the couple emerge as parents and the baby is well on the way to getting used to her new life.

With visitors excluded, Mom, Dad, and baby can think of nothing else but themselves and their new life together. No energy is lost on visitors, and Mom gets to rest while perfecting breast-feeding.

Do you remember…?

Remember how you use to cradle your own babies on your shoulder, rock them in your arms, or pat them on your knee? These ways of handling a baby may come back to you the minute you hold a new grandchild in your arms, and you'll find yourself instinctively rocking back and forth with your precious bundle. But some of us may feel a little nervous at first when holding a baby again, so here are some tips to refresh your memory and restore your confidence:

Shoulder hold

Remember this one? Hold the baby with her head resting on your shoulder. Check that her head is well supported and then pat her back gently with your free hand. Babies love this position and it also helps with burping.

Cradle hold

Hold your grandchild in your arms with her head in the crook of your elbow and your free hand supporting her back. Start rocking her gently from side to side and you'll find yourself rhythmically moving from foot to foot, just like you used to.

Overarm hold

I'm sure you know this one too. Lie the baby face down over your forearm and then move slowly around, patting her gently on the back. You can also use this hold sitting down with the baby on your lap. Sit with the baby face-down over your lap and again gently pat her on the back. This is a great way of soothing a crying or colicky baby.

Shoulder hold

Cradle hold

Overarm hold

"*Always remember that the best gift for any grandchild is time*"

"I don't see my grandchildren enough"

Karen is 58 and has two young grandchildren. Her worry is that she doesn't get to see them as often as she'd like. Her daughter and son-in-law were very firm about visiting from the start: when their first baby was born they told everyone there were to be no visitors since they wanted to bond as a family. Karen didn't get to see her grandsons for two weeks, which she found very hard. Ever since, they've made it clear that she can only visit by invitation. It's not often enough for Karen and she's upset.

her family became more comfortable with her and she saw them more often. Now, as long as she gives some warning, Grandma can visit more or less as much as she likes.

I would urge Karen to be patient. Seeing her grandchildren now and then is better than not seeing them at all. She'll only become an irritant if she keeps on hassling them. Parents have a right to bring their children up the way they want to, and grandparents have to accept that. Karen has to look at things from her children's point of view and not just from her own.

> I'd suggest that Karen doesn't press for more visits but makes the most of the ones she has. Perhaps she could take the grandchildren out sometimes to give Mom a break

I have a friend who found herself in the much the same situation as Karen and she felt slighted too. But she came to realize that her son and daughter-in-law wanted to live their lives in their own way, and that was to keep themselves to themselves.

My friend decided to show them she could be a hands-off grandma, and she did her best to be pleasant and to accept them as they were. She bit her tongue before criticizing—although there were plenty of things she wanted to criticize. Little by little,

It may be painful, but she has to accept the conditions her daughter and son-in-law prefer. She has no option if she wants to see her grandchild. So I wouldn't press for more invitations but make the most of the visits she has. I suggest that Karen shows what an asset she can be to them and makes offers to help. Perhaps she could take the grandchildren off their hands sometimes and give Mom and Dad an afternoon off? I would advise Karen to take things slowly and hopefully everyone will benefit.

3 *Your Grandchild's Food*

From breast- or bottle-feeding to solid-food choices, food can be a tricky topic for parents, and one where your experience can be a real help.

Breast is best

Breast or bottle is one of the first, and most important, decisions a new mother has to make. She has the right to make up her own mind and, whatever her choice, your most valuable role is to help make life as easy and pleasant as possible for her and your grandchild during those first weeks and months, so that they both thrive.

Best for Mom, best for Baby

There's no question that breast-feeding is best. There are so many benefits for both mother and baby, and scientists and doctors now know much more about the importance of these. In the US, numbers have increaased with 75 percent of mothers breast-feeding at birth and 22 percent at a year (this includes babies getting any breast milk. The rate of exclusive breast-feeding at 6 months is 13 percent).

If your daughter is thinking of stopping breast-feeding because of problems getting the baby to feed or because breast-feeding is painful, your support could make a world of difference and give her the fortitude to continue. It might be very useful to be aware of the latest research on the importance of breast-feeding to give you the confidence to encourage her, so I'm listing the major benefits here.

Be careful, though—it would be unkind to dwell on these in a way that would undermine your bottle-feeding daughter. The guiding principle of grandparents should be always to back up your daughter and son, whatever their choices. The vast majority of babies thrive with whatever approach to feeding is followed, so it's never worth making a fuss and trying to go against what your children decide.

Give her support
For some moms, breast-feeding goes smoothly right from the start, but there can be difficulties at first. Support your daughter in her efforts and do everything you can to give her confidence during these first days.

Benefits for Baby

Perfect nutrition Mother's milk provides the exact nutrients needed for the first six months of life.

Stronger immune system Breast milk contains antibodies to every infection the mother has ever suffered and passes protection against them to the baby. Breast milk also contains good bacteria (probiotics), which stimulate the baby's immune system to fight infection from the first feeding.

Better weaning Breast milk contains a growth factor that prepares a baby's digestive system for solid food.

Brain boost Breast milk contains omega-3 fatty acids to build a baby's rapidly developing brain and eyes.

Sleep easier Breast milk contains chemicals that soothe babies and promote sleep.

Healthier eating Research suggests that babies who are breast-fed are less likely to be obese in childhood.

Better long-term health Studies show that being breast-fed reduces the risk of developing allergies, asthma, and childhood diabetes.

Benefits for Mom

Lower cancer risk Research shows breast-feeding helps to protect against both breast cancer and ovarian cancer.

Less post-baby weight Breast-feeding moms burn an extra 500 calories a day. Breast-feeding also releases a hormone, oxytocin, that stimulates Mom's uterus to contract, so her belly get its shape back more quickly. And contrary to popular belief, breast-feeding doesn't leave breasts droopy—that's a result of pregnancy itself.

No microwave required Wherever Mom is, breast milk is instantly ready.

More spare cash The parents can save around $1000 a year on formula.

Better bonding During breast-feeding, a mom and her baby both produce oxytocin, known as the "love hormone," so they become closer, physically and emotionally.

Healthier heart Studies show that breast-feeding can reduce the mother's risk of a heart attack by a quarter.

Stronger bones Women who breast-feed are three-quarters less likely to develop the bone-thinning disease osteoporosis. They lose a small amount of bone mass during nursing but, after weaning, the body replaces it with new, denser bone.

Long-term health A new Swedish study has also found women who breast-feed for up to 12 months are a quarter less likely to develop rheumatoid arthritis.

An update on breast-feeding

If you breast-fed your own children, what I'm going to say will be second nature to you, but a refresher may be helpful. If, however, you bottle-fed your babies, and in the 1970s and 80s a lot of us did, you might need some information to help you support and encourage your daughter.

Some moms don't get the help they need

One thing to bear in mind is that many new mothers miss out on the specialized instruction they need in order start breast-feeding. The average stay on a labor ward nowadays is less than two days and, in my experience, many new mothers require three days at least to master breast-feeding. After such a short hospital stay, they may return home feeling insecure about their ability to breast-feed.

"You can help by encouraging your daughter to put her feet up and rest while she's getting breast-feeding established"

Due to a shortage of lactation consultants on postpartum floors and the limited time of nurses to help establish breast-feeding, some new moms may have a hard time getting their baby to nurse effectively. However, lactation consultants are available after discharge from the hospital, and may be covered by insurance. Organizations like La Leche League can also provide support.

And some new moms may feel pressure from other moms and even from husbands. Many women decide during pregnancy not to breast-feed. Talking to other moms at childbirth classes, you can get the impression that most moms

Do you remember...?

If you breast-fed, do you remember finding it hard to get the baby to latch on well? I see some moms with babies who are hardly on the breast, and not surprisingly the baby can't suck properly and get milk. And as you know, if milk isn't drawn off the breasts frequently, they quickly stop producing milk.

If your daughter is having problems, encourage her to get the baby latched on properly, with the whole nipple *and* areola in the baby's mouth. Then the breasts can be emptied when the baby smacks his tongue against the hard palate of his mouth. You might also like to show your daughter how to keep her breasts full while the baby's feeding by gently squeezing the body of the breast during breaks between nursing. The more a baby nurses, the more milk the breasts will produce.

are going to bottle feed and the easy option is to go along with them. It's a fact that some fathers can be nervous about breast-feeding, and that's difficult for a mom to handle. If your daughter is going to breast-feed, you can do her a big favor by supporting her, even if her partner's not in favor. Perhaps you can help to bring him around to her way of thinking?

Help her rest

Another way you can help your daughter is by encouraging her to rest. Looking after a new baby takes it out of her, so doing some of the household jobs, like making meals or loading the dishwasher, helps keep her breast milk flowing.

Every mom needs a baby who is eager to feed, and a bit of luck to get breast-feeding going in the first week after the birth. It has to be said that girl babies tend to get the knack quicker than boys. Boys sometimes need more patience and more coaxing. Babies need feeding often during these early days so this can be an ideal time to help your daughter and grandchild learn the all-important trick of latching on—if she asks for your advice, of course.

Misunderstood colostrum

Help her rest
It's important for a new mom to rest as much as possible during the first few weeks of breast-feeding. If you can help with household tasks, you'll help her stay relaxed.

Before the creamy breast milk "comes in," at about 72 hours after the birth, the breasts produce colostrum, a clear golden liquid, which looks thin. Despite its appearance, it's the ideal food for a newborn baby making the transition to dealing with food by mouth for the first time. If the weak-looking colostrum is a reason your daughter feels she can't persist with breast-feeding you can reassure her of its nutritious quality.

Do you remember sore nipples?

Women now are luckier than we were—they have access to more information and detailed scientific research about the best ways to get breastfeeding started, and avoid problems such as sore nipples.

If, despite these, your daughter's nipples do get sore, even cracked, have a quiet talk and see if you can help. As you know, nipples can get sore for two main reasons: first, the baby's mouth is pulled off the breast, stretching the delicate skin; second, the baby is allowed to suck and chew on the breast while not really feeding. You'll probably remember that the solution to the first is to break the airtight seal between the baby's mouth and the breast by gently inserting a little finger in the corner of the baby's mouth. And for the second, take the baby off the breast as soon as he stops real feeding. A third reason can be that the baby is not latched on properly so tactfully suggest your daughter checks her position.

" *Remember how you break the seal between the baby's mouth and the breast with your little finger?* "

Supply and demand

Your daughter may have no problems with breast-feeding. But just in case, and so you're not tempted to nag her about her feeding regimen, you might like a few reminders about how breast-feeding works.

The rigid feeding regimen so popular today may be partly responsible for fewer and fewer mothers breast-feeding their babies beyond six weeks. It may actually be pushing mothers toward bottle-feeding. You could use your influence to help your daughter believe in herself and her ability to breast-feed her baby—to trust her breasts, in fact. The right way to think about it is that the baby and breast are a team—a baby knows what's best for the breasts.

Breasts will only produce a good supply of milk if it is drawn off frequently, that is if the baby is feeding often. The flow of milk is therefore successfully established if a baby is given the breast whenever she seems hungry—in the first week this can be every one to two hours. If milk stays in the breast for much longer—for three or four hours—breasts stop making milk. So a strict by-the-clock feeding regimen depresses milk production, and so does making a baby wait to be fed.

Thereafter follows a sad train of events. The milk appears to dry up. A mother, fearing she isn't making enough milk and worrying that her baby will go hungry and not gain weight, unnecessarily abandons breast-feeding and switches to bottles and formula.

How you can help in the first few days

A really contented baby is one who is fed ad lib—when he wants to feed—in the first couple of weeks. It may, on the face of it, seem tiring for Mom, but having a baby who cries little, settles easily, and sleeps much of the time is worth the sacrifice. For this reason, many moms like to maintain skin-to-skin contact (Mom lies in a semireclining position and baby lies face down on her belly and chest) for the first three days so a baby can feed hourly if he wants, even if Mom is snoozing! I know you might be worried about this, but as long as your daughter is careful and aware of the risks, I'm all in favor.

Leave her in peace
Giving a new mom the space and time to rest while she nurses her baby is one of the greatest gifts you can offer her. You can make sure she's not disturbed by phone calls or visitors.

Keeping blood sugar steady

With the baby sleeping in a crib, separate from his mother, there tends to be intervals of two or three hours between feedings, which are long intervals to a baby. Such long intervals go hand in hand with a low blood sugar. A newborn baby's brain is exceedingly sensitive to the level of blood sugar and if it drops, the baby will be fretful, cry a lot, wake frequently from sleep, and be difficult to settle down. An infant who nurses from the breast—not from a bottle—will use the fats in the mother's milk to keep blood-sugar levels steady.

For the baby's sake, the goal of everyone taking care of a mother and newborn baby should be to minimize the intervals between feedings and keep the baby's blood sugar steady. This will happen quite naturally if the newborn baby is allowed to lie on the reclining mother's abdomen and chest and nurse at will. You can see that a baby lying in a crib can't follow his natural instinct, only feeding at two or three hourly intervals when he alerts you by crying or when an adult sees fit. This baby will run the danger of having low blood sugar, which in itself irritates the brain and will cause deep distress and a lot of crying.

Feeding on demand is only slightly better than feeding by the clock. Demand feeding means waiting for the baby to cry—due to the discomfort of low blood sugar—which, by necessity, is waiting too long. For the first few days by far the best way is continuous feeding.

To me, this knife-edge need of the newborn baby's brain to keep levels of blood sugar steady is an incontrovertible argument against those who try to impose a clock-watching approach to infant feeding.

> **" *Keeping the house and family running over during these first few days is a precious gift from you to her, and one neither of you will forget* "**

This is extremely demanding for your daughter, and your help can be invaluable if she asks for it. She needs feeding and being taken care of almost like a baby herself. She needs to let everything except herself and her baby go. Keeping the house and family running over during these first few days is a precious gift from you to her, and one neither of you will forget.

You might find helping out like this very tiring, but bear in mind that you have such a short window of opportunity here—your grandchild will grow up so fast. Perhaps this thought will give you that little extra bit of energy.

Supporting your daughter

If your daughter has opted to breast-feed, she needs all the help and support she can get. For one thing breast-feeding is very tiring. The body, and the breasts in particular, use a lot of calories making the milk, so a breast-feeding woman needs about 500 additional calories each to deal with those energy requirements.

What you can do

Making milk consumes a lot of water, so it's easy for a breast-feeding woman to get dehydrated, especially while the baby's on the breast. She literally loses fluid to feed her baby and needs a great deal of water to drink. So you can be both useful and thoughtful by bringing her glasses of water while she's nursing to quench her thirst.

Added to this kind of exhaustion is sleep deprivation due to nighttime feedings and getting up in the night to change and settle the baby. So a breast-feeding woman can get totally exhausted in a matter of a few weeks. I remember well one of my daughters, who was breast-feeding twin girls, looking ashen white and expressionless with fatigue. When the twins were eight weeks old I begged her to stop for fear of her health. Sometimes Mom's welfare just has to come first for the sake of the whole family.

Helping physically

Anything you can do to relieve your daughter and son of physical effort will be greatly appreciated. You don't have to look for specific jobs, just taking on some chores will score a bull's-eye. So it's not that different than what you do in your

own home. Check with your daughter or son first and find out what would be most useful. Helpful tasks could be:

- Loading and unloading the dishwasher or doing dishes and putting everything away
- Sorting the laundry and doing a couple of loads
- Transferring the washed clothes and getting the drier going
- Folding the clothes and putting them away
- Bringing tea, water, or juice
- Cooking a simple meal
- Tidying up, dusting, vacuuming
- Jotting down a shopping list and doing the shopping
- Bathing the baby
- Feeding expressed milk to the baby.

"You can be of enormous support by just being steady as a rock, unflappable, patient, and sympathetic. You've been there and you know what it's like"

Helping emotionally

Very few moms get through the first month without a few tears (the baby blues) and some emotional upheaval. That can leave her shaken and insecure about herself.

You can be of enormous support just by being steady as a rock, being unflappable, patient, and sympathetic. After all, you've been there so you can say with complete sincerity that you understand what your daughter and son are feeling and what they're going through.

Remember how nervous you felt with your first baby. You longed for praise, reassurance, and encouragement. Well now you're in the position to give those things to the next generation.

It will mean such a lot to them both if you can find things to praise. That isn't difficult, there's always something you'll see your daughter and son doing that deserves congratulation. Your role is primarily to be a fan (not a coach or manager) so encouraging things to say might be:

- I think you make great parents
- I think you're both doing a great job
- You're a good mom/dad
- I wish I'd done that with my baby (or babies)
- That's such a good idea
- That works very well, doesn't it?
- I love the way you…
- More moms/dads should be like you
- What a lucky baby she is to have you as her mom/dad.

Help where you can Any kind of help will be welcome in these early days. Be ready to make coffee for visitors, help older siblings with their homework, and empty the dishwasher— whatever is needed.

Helping socially

Taking your new grandchild for walks and outings will bring you great pleasure. So suggest giving Mom and Dad some time on their own by taking the baby out of the house and relieving them of responsibility for a while.

And you can give them precious time out by offering to babysit and give a late feeding too, so they can enjoy a night out as a couple. Your daughter can express her milk to cover the feedings while she's out of the house.

> **" Bottle-feeding with expressed milk allows Grandma or Dad to enjoy that closeness "**

Your daughter may appreciate some moral support when she sees her pediatrician, so offer to be with her or accompany her. And you might be a useful extra pair of hands and eyes when she goes to a mothers' group. This will also give you the opportunity to meet some of her friends who are new moms.

Supporting your son

Your son could be feeling a bit left out in these early days after the birth. Everyone, including you, is concentrating on the baby and Mom. Here you have the perfect opportunity to help and support your son while indirectly supporting your daughter.

When your daughter is resting or sleeping you and your son can do things together to support Team Baby. While sharing the chores, you'll have a good chance to chat, and perhaps he'll open up and express his feelings about his role, even his insecurities, while you're working together.

You can give him invaluable feedback about how good a dad and husband he's being. You can ask how he thinks you can best help him and, having learned he can trust you, he may be inclined to give you free range.

Enjoy bottle-feeding
Don't worry if your daughter does decide to bottle-feed—your grandchild will still thrive. And it means that you can enjoy giving lots of feedings yourself.

You can help your breast-feeding daughter by getting her partner on board about her maternal role. Research shows that having a supportive partner is the key factor in helping moms persevere with breast-feeding. Help him understand that there are plenty of ways he can be involved, including taking over some feedings himself with expressed milk. Encourage him by being his biggest fan and keeping the praise coming.

If it's bottles...

Mother's milk is important to your grandchild, but it's not as important as her love. If your daughter does decide to bottle-feed, do everything you can to support her and help her not feel guilty about it. Help her make sure that the baby has the same attention and closeness at feeding times as he would have if she were breast-feeding.

Getting Dad involved

One of the good things about bottle-feeding is that the new father can be just as involved as Mom at feeding times, especially if he feeds the baby as soon as possible after the birth. This way he can get used to the technique and won't be afraid to handle the baby. As it happens, the sooner he learns to do all the things that the baby needs, the better. And he'll bond with his newborn baby if he opens his shirt when giving a bottle so that the baby nestles up to his skin as he is feeding and bonds with his father's smell. It's useful for you, as a grandparent, to understand all this so you can encourage your son.

There's a payoff for grandparents too if your grandchild is being bottle-fed—you can help by giving some feedings and enjoy that wonderful closeness yourself. Grandparents or Dad can take the baby out, with feeding equipment, without having to worry about rushing home for a feeding.

Even bottle-feeding changes

The majority of babies will have a bottle at some stage—if not continuously right from the start, then often after introducing solids or with supplementary bottles, so it's good to know what to do. You may think you know all about bottle-feeding and it will be just the same as in your day, but think again. New infant formulas, bottles, and nipples appear on the market regularly, all with the goal of making bottle-feeding as convenient and as similar to breast-feeding as possible.

Some of the hygiene advice has remained the same. It is still considered fine to make up a batch of formula as long as it is stored in the refrigerator and used within 24 hours of making up the bottle.

If your grandchild is being bottle-fed, check with your daughter and son about how the bottles are to be made up and follow their instructions to the letter. Practice making up a bottle so you're ready if you're asked to babysit.

Remember that, just as with breast-feeding, it is vital to keep the baby's blood sugar steady. If it drops, the baby will cry and be fretful (see page 49).

Bottles and nipples

There's a wide range of different bottles and nipples now available and your daughter and son will experiment to find what suits their baby best. Disposable bottles are now available, which can be very useful when traveling or, for example, if you have the baby at your house for an afternoon and you don't have all the sterilizing equipment. Disposables come sterilized and have a nipple and lid, so all you need to do is add formula.

Ready-to-use formula

This is another godsend for grandparents. The formula comes in a carton, ready to be poured into a sterile bottle. This is a perfect solution if you are out and about with your grandchild or taking care of him at your house.

Sterilizing equipment

You will remember how important it is for every bit of feeding equipment to be carefully cleaned after use to protect babies from infection. It's not enough just to wash equipment—it must also be sterilized, and there are several ways of doing this. Popular methods include boiling or using a cold-water sterilizing unit or a steam sterilizer. Ask your daughter to show you how to use the system she's chosen so you can help if needed, but here is some background information.

"If your grandchild is being bottle-fed, check with your daughter and son about how bottles are to be made up and follow their instructions to the letter"

With cold-water sterilizing units, bottles can be left in the solution until needed. Before using a bottle, shake off any excess solution from both the bottle and the nipple, or rinse with cooled, boiled water. If you are using a steam sterilizer, equipment should be re-sterilized before you use it, if it's not going to be used immediately after sterilizing.

Equipment can also be sterilized in the microwave using a specially designed steam unit, as long as the feeding equipment is suitable for microwave use. Once a baby starts to play on the floor for any length of time, the sterilizing routine can be relaxed, and bottles and other equipment can be cleaned thoroughly, then washed in the dishwasher.

Making up the bottles

You might not need to do this, but it's good to be up to date on current thinking just in case you do need to. The advice now is to make up one bottle at a time. Bacteria multiply quickly and making bottles up in advance increases the risk of infection.

You'll remember how important it is to wash your hands and check that everything is clean. You may find your daughter has a sterilizing spray to ensure your hands and the work surfaces are scrupulously clean.

- Check all the surfaces are clean and wash your hands
- Use only batches made less than 24 hours ago and that have been refrigerated.
- Boil water in a kettle, and allow to cool to 158 °F
- Put the correct amount of water in the bottle, then add the right amount of formula
- Shake the bottle to mix, then cool under a running faucet until a test splash on your wrist feels neither hot or cold.

Giving bottles—remember how you used to...?

It may be a while since you've fed a young baby with a bottle, but it will all come back to you. Just in case, here are a few reminders:

- Hold the baby with his head slightly raised so he can breathe and swallow safely and there's no risk of choking.
- Gently put the nipple in his mouth and don't push it too far back. When he begins to suck, hold the bottle at an angle to keep the nipple full of formula and free of air.
- If your grandchild wants to keep on sucking when the bottle is empty, gently slide your little finger between his gums to encourage him to let go.

easure the formula carefully   Test the temperature   Put the nipple into his mouth

Solids

Advice on when to introduce solids to a baby has swung back and forth over the years. The World Health Organization's recommendation has been to begin at six months, but this is now being questioned by child nutrition experts, who say that starting at four to six months is acceptable.

Catch up with the latest advice

The debate on starting solids will continue but, in the end, it comes down to common sense when you're dealing with a hungry baby. There is a lot of confusing advice out there. But the American Academy of Pediatricians recommends introducing solids at 4 months for formula-fed babies and 6 months for breast-fed babies. It further recommends continuing to breast-feed in addition to solid foods for at least the first year of life and for longer depending on the mom's preference.

Happy mealtimes
Once your grandchild is on solids, you'll love helping feed her and you can make it fun for both of you.

As with all other aspects of your grandchild's life, the decision on when to introduce solids is up to your daughter and son. It's important, though, to be aware of current advice so you're not tempted to try and get them to start solids earlier.

The reasons for this are quite clear: a baby's digestive system isn't well-developed enough to digest solids under four months, giving rise to two things no one wants: a baby's tummy will get upset and the solids fail to nourish the baby. The advice given by manufacturers has never been brought into line with the AAP advice.

The BFI (Baby Friendly Initiative) goes even further than the AAP. It suggests that women should continue breast-feeding way beyond six months, up to two years, in conjunction with giving solid food.

Options for introducing solids

Your role is to support your children in whatever they decide to do. They have several options to choose from, none particularly better than another.

To purée or not to purée? Single foods or mixed? Spoon-feeding or self-feeding? Starting a baby on solids has become something of a minefield in recent years. No wonder new research has found that many moms are confused about what to do and which foods are appropriate, and you may be too.

For example, nearly half of moms think that green leafy vegetables and chicken are no-gos, when in fact they're ideal foods for babies of about seven months. The problem is that these sorts of misconceptions can lead to moms not giving their children a nutritionally balanced diet. Babies need to be fed a whole variety of different foods in the first year to ensure they get all the nutrients they require and don't become picky eaters. The thing to remember is that the goal of starting solids is to get the baby on to the same diet as the rest of the family, so mashed potatoes with juices from the meat are fine, as are family soups and desserts—as long as they don't contain salt or sugar.

I'm a great believer in child-led introduction of solids. This means simply giving babies "finger foods" and allowing them to master eating for themselves. With this method, babies get to choose what they eat and decide when they are full—rather than being spoon-fed by Mom.

Research shows babies fed in this way rarely become obese or fussy or suffer from eating disorders such as anorexia. It also allows babies to join in family meals and makes feeding battles less likely.

When to introduce solids?

It's your daughter's decision, but there's no harm in you keeping a lookout for these signs that your grandchild is ready to start solids:

- She can sit up unsupported
- She reaches out to grasp objects and put them in her mouth
- She shows great interest in food.

Say no to:

If you are preparing any foods for your grandchild, your daughter will want you to say no to:

Salt Never add any salt to the foods you give your baby grandchild, because her kidneys can't manage it.

Sugar Sugary foods and drinks aren't recommended for babies under two years, since they can encourage a sweet tooth and lead to decay when teeth come in.

What's healthy for babies now

Since our time, what's considered healthy food for babies has changed quite a lot. Both salt and sugar are no-nos and they're never added to children's food from baby food right through to the teenage years. This is for good reasons so never be tempted to go against your daughter's wishes. You won't be doing your grandchild any favors if you do.

Water is best

Some healthy foods such as pure fruit juices are still high in sugar, and I believe that any fruit juice should be diluted by one part to four with water for the first year, and one in two after that. By far the healthiest option, though, is to encourage a baby to drink only water. Once this habit is established water can be the standard drink up to five years old; carbonated water can then be the treat, not sugar-filled fruit drinks and sodas. The no-sugar, no-salt rule shouldn't only apply to babies. It should extend right through toddlerhood, so don't give your grandchild sugary things as treats.

More fruit and vegetables

Preparing meals
Making baby's lunch is a great way to help your daughter. And you'll be very popular if you prepare fruit and vegetable purées and take them over to pop into the freezer, ready to use when needed.

People of all ages are encouraged to eat five servings of fruit and vegetables a day and that applies to babies being starting solids too. Five a day seems on the conservative side to me and babies can easily take more if they're offered fruit and vegetables at each meal, both during and after starting on solids.

We used to start solids with wheat cereal. Nowadays most moms will start with a rice cereal and will add meals of puréed fruit and vegetables fairly quickly. So by two weeks into solids your grandchild could be having cereal for breakfast, puréed vegetable for lunch, and puréed fruit for dinner.

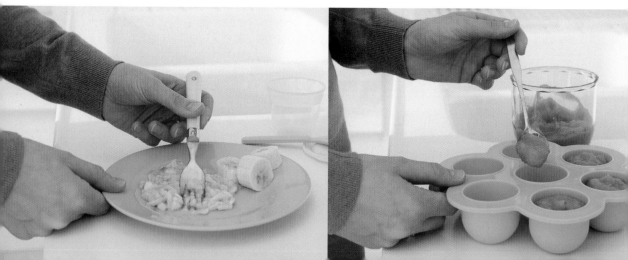

I like the modern way of puréeing a quantity of a single vegetable or fruit and filling ice trays. This way frozen cubes of fruit and vegetables can be defrosted and served in minutes. A few weeks into solids, one cube will be a good meal. The same can be done with single fruits. And you'd be really helping your daughter out if you offered to do some cooking and puréeing to make a batch of these frozen cubes for her.

By the age of seven to eight months, babies should be having lots of protein because they're growing so quickly. Eggs, chicken, and fish are good, as well as red meat—babies need iron. At this age there's no need to purée meat and fish. Babies are ready for new textures and love "gumming" food. It's good for babies to be given morsels of fish, chicken, and meat to chew on to relish the flavors. Even if your grandchild spits out the protein he still gets nutrition from the juices.

> *" It's good for babies to be given morsels of fish, chicken, and meat to chew on to relish the flavors "*

How to encourage healthy eating early

An appetite for healthy food starts while a baby is still in the uterus. No, really. And your daughter can start early, when her baby is growing inside her. The flavors of the foods she eats cross the placenta and emerge in the liquid that surrounds her baby. Her unborn baby actually sips the liquid and acquires a taste for the foods mom is eating! Her baby will love those same healthy foods when he's fed them later as part of his mixed feeding. There's plenty of research evidence to support this.

She can also encourage her baby to get a taste for healthy food while she's breast-feeding. Eating healthy foods herself means the flavors are present in her milk and her baby gets to love them. Babies interpret anything that's in breast milk as being good to eat. So when those foods they've tasted in mom's milk are fed to them when starting solids, their early experience guides babies to eat them eagerly.

Eat greens first

Once your grandchild is eating different foods, a healthy habit is to give vegetables first when she's really hungry to ensure she eats them before starting on protein and starches. Fruit can be given at the end of a meal as a dessert.

I used to advise moms to try a new food for only three days before finding an alternative if their baby kept refusing it—until I read some interesting research. Dr. Andrea Mayer at the Nestlé Nutrition Research Institute in Switzerland found that babies who refuse a food day after day will often take it by the 11th or 12th day. So it's worth persevering with a really nutritious food such as broccoli a lot longer than a week.

What's the latest on allergies?

Delicious!
It's good to let a baby feed herself as soon as she is able. She'll enjoy it and it will help her manual dexterity. But you will remember that she must never be left alone with food in case she chokes.

We didn't worry about allergies nearly as much as modern-day moms do, so it's important for you to know about the latest advice on baby foods that could potentially cause an allergy. A global consensus of allergy specialists agree it's a good idea to introduce all the foods that might cause allergies, one at the time, from six months, starting with just a small amount. This includes eggs, whole

milk, and wheat (and other cereals that contain gluten, such as barley and oats). By the end of the first year your grandchild should have eaten all potentially allergic foods. Introducing them before the end of the first year has been shown to lower the chances of a food allergy developing later.

What about peanuts?

A decade ago peanut allergy was very rare, but cases have tripled in the past 10 years. Infant allergy expert Dr. Carina Venter, of the University of Portsmouth, says there's no need for pregnant women from nonallergic families to avoid peanuts. However, she does advise that pregnant women from families in which there is a peanut allergy may want to consider avoiding them and peanut-containing products.

It's interesting that peanut allergy is virtually unknown in African countries, where peanuts are used as a first solid food. It's possible that delaying giving peanuts to our children actually encourages peanut allergy.

"No job should be too menial if you want to be one of the family. So my advice is to be on the lookout for small jobs that need doing and offer to take them on"

Practical things you can do to help

Two of the most useful roles you can take on for your son and daughter are mother's helper and sous chef. Both roles require you to ask how you can best give a hand, and a good way is to say something like, "Can I help you out with that?" or, "What can I do that would help you the most?"

You may get the reply, "Would you be an angel and fold the laundry—put it all in that large basket." or, "Could you chop the tomatoes and onions for the pasta sauce, and, yes I'd love it if you cooked it and put it in those containers for the freezer."

No job should be too menial if you want to be one of the family. So my advice is to be on the lookout for small jobs that need doing and offer to take them on. Every little thing can be a help to a mom with a baby or small children. In the evening you could offer to cook or order in a meal. You'll be Number One Grandma if you're able to give Mom and Dad a break with a cup of coffee, or play with the baby while your daughter checks her emails or catches 40 winks.

You can also help by falling in with the household habits. Many parents these days are much more concerned with what their child eats than where and when he eats it, and grandparents can sometimes be disapproving of this approach. If you are one of these, I'd advise you to resist the temptation to interfere and go along with whatever works for them. No child is harmed by happy eating.

Baby takes charge

Many parents now are in favor of self-feeding—allowing the baby to select for herself from an array of finger foods. I love this new approach, and I think there are lots of advantages. Feeding herself helps a baby's self-esteem, and don't worry—she will make sure she gets enough to eat.

Encourage do-it-yourself feeding

If your daughter breast- or bottle-feeds up to six months, your grandchild will have developed sufficiently to feed herself. She can pick up food, she can get it to her mouth, and she can "gum" it.

The goal is to get the baby to feed herself as soon as she can pick up and hold food. If a child chooses her own pieces of food, she is more likely to eat them than if you hand them to her. Babies stop eating when they're full, while a mother spooning food into her child's mouth will often overeat.

“ The goal is to get the baby to feed herself as soon as she can pick up and hold food ”

What's behind baby-led feeding

As a grandparent, you might be worried by this idea, but let me reassure you. I'm a big advocate of baby-led feeding for two very good reasons, one medical and the other social: it counteracts childhood obesity and prevents fussy eating.

Babies who feed themselves from six months onward eat until they've had enough and no more. Babies who are spoon-fed run the risk of having more food than they want or need from adults eager for them to finish.

Babies who choose foods for themselves are more likely to try new foods and to eat healthy foods if offered to them. You therefore avoid problems with getting a child to eat vegetables and fruit when they're older.

It's good for your grandchild

A six-month-old baby has no need to start with puréed solids before graduating to food with lumps. They already have all the equipment to feed themselves with easy-to-hold pieces of meat, fish, cheese, fruit, and vegetables. First they suck them, then "gum" them, and finally they chew them when the first teeth arrive.

Being fed from a spoon is redundant for most six-month-old babies. In the first place spoon-feeding is a difficult transition for a baby to make after sucking from a breast or bottle where milk is sucked to the back of the mouth. Solids are best maneuvered around the front of the mouth for chewing or gumming and this happens only when a baby self-feeds.

One of the strongest arguments for baby-led feeding is that it's fun for the baby and it stokes up her sense of achievement and self-esteem. Using a spoon her holds him back and deprives her of this boost.

Is your grandchild ready for baby-led feeding?

Reassure yourself by helping your daughter look out for these signs that show your grandchild is ready to start feeding herself. As you will remember, never leave her alone with finger foods to prevent choking.

- She can sit in her high chair unsupported
- She holds toys and puts them in her mouth
- She can sit up without assistance
- She picks up food and puts it in her mouth
- She chews on her fingers and other objects
- She shows a great interest in food.

A six-month-old baby is developmentally ready to self-feed. Look for the following:

- Good hand-eye coordination
- A primitive kind of grasp with which to pick up and hold food
- A determination to put everything in her mouth, so why not healthy food?

What does your grandchild good

Long before we knew what makes some foods better for us than others, we got by. We may not have always eaten the healthiest of diets, but nonetheless some of us are living well beyond our biblical lifespan of three score years and ten. I survived the lean war years in England, when it's said we ate a healthier diet than many people eat now. The deprivation was good for us and we had to concentrate on foods that were really nutritious.

More aware

Nowadays most moms and dads are pretty obsessive about giving their children simple and nutritious food, home cooked whenever possible, and free of salt, sugar, and fat. Today's moms and dads know much more than we did about what's in different foods, what makes them especially good for babies, and why certain foods have to be eaten every day by growing children.

"Modern parents are more adventurous about food than we were and look further afield to include more exotic fruit and vegetables that provide important nutrients"

More adventurous

What also distinguishes the younger generation is that they're more adventurous about food then we ever were. So while we may have strained or mashed vegetables for our babies when introducing solids, we probably restricted ourselves to root vegetables like carrots, potatoes, and parsnips, and fruit like apples, pears, and bananas—all good in their way but bland after a while.

Modern parents look further afield to include more exotic fruits and vegetables,and for good reason, because most of them provide nutrients not found in the more traditional varieties. So moms will include yellow and orange fruit and vegetables such as pumpkin/squash, sweet potatoes, peaches, mangoes, and papayas not only because they're interesting but also because they contain carotene (vitamin A) a potent antioxidant and health giver. Tofu is an ideal first food; most babies love it and it's packed with protein. Avocados contain essential fatty acids for a baby's growing brain and eyes, and its consistency makes it an ideal first food.

New ways

Parents today will also give first foods in a slightly different way from us. From seven or eight months all of my grandchildren have loved sucking on carrot sticks dipped in hummus held in their tiny hands, cucumber in easy-to-hold-sticks to slurp on, and pear and apple wedges. Children adore choosing what they eat; it gives them self-confidence and the pride of achievement. So my sons and daughters have wisely just spread out a variety of foods, in shapes a baby's hand can deal with, on the clean high-chair tray and let the baby decide what he eats. By serving vegetables for the first five minutes when a baby is most hungry, you will ensure he eats a day's quota. Then comes the protein course with small pieces of egg, chicken, meat, fish, cheese, and tofu, then small pieces of fruit and berries to finish. A child who eats like this will know when to stop and will never be fat.

So the days of sitting with a dish and spoon could be a thing of the past. And that's not a bad thing. Spoon-feeding adults tend to get babies to finish what *they* think is a reasonable portion and they may not be right. Remember, a portion is what a baby can hold in the palm of his hand.

New combinations

Just open any book on infant feeding and you'll find endless recipes for making first foods interesting. This doesn't mean flavoring them artificially or putting more than one food together with another. It's important that foods are given separately for the first few months of solids so that a baby learns and relishes individual flavors, tastes, and textures. Despite there being jars for babies of spaghetti marinara and lamb stew, these kind of mixtures should be reserved for emergencies.

Try new foods
Many babies love new tastes so don't hesitate to offer her different foods, such as mango and papaya. And if your grandchild doesn't take to something the first time, keep trying.

However you can give carrot a bit of zip with orange zest, add a drop or two of apple juice to another fruit, or from around 10 months add a dash of cumin to a soup or other vegetable dish. Adding a little yogurt to a puréed green vegetable like spinach, zucchini, or broccoli can help it slip down easily during early introduction of first foods.

Children love carrot sticks

Feeding Grandma is fun too

Broccoli is a superfood

Great baby foods

(Serve as purées until your grandchild can pick them up himself.)

Broccoli A must: contains calcium for growing bones and iron for blood.

Carrots Children love them and they are a great source of vitamin A.

Peas, beans, and legumes Packed with plant proteins and B vitamins; chickpeas and lentils are especially good; baked beans are fine, as long as they're low in sugar and salt.

Tomatoes Cut into wedges for your grandchild to suck on. The juice contains a lot of vitamin C and lycopene, a powerful antioxidant.

Apples Leave the peel on: most of the goodness is just under the skin.

Berries The darker the better, like blueberries, squashed to avoid the risk of choking. They're fun for him to pick up and pop in his mouth.

Grapefruit and orange wedges Full of vitamin C and supernutrients.

Eggs (after 6 months) Hugely nutritious, with all the B vitamins, including B12 for brain and nerve growth.

Oatmeal Get started early so your grandchild will eat this superfood throughout his life, since it lowers cholesterol.

Pitted Olives From the time they could pick them up, all my grandchildren loved olives—a good source of vitamin E and essential fats.

Prunes Soft and juicy to suck on, a rich source of iron, and good for bowel health.

Whole grains (after 6 months) Cereals, bread, and pasta for fiber, roughage, and B vitamins.

Pomegranate juice Dilute one part juice to four parts water for up to 12 months, one part juice to two parts water thereafter.

Meals with the family

I'm sure you remember how much your own children loved to be involved with the rest of the family at mealtimes. Encourage your daughter to do the same and help your grandchild enjoy mealtimes.

Joining in

As soon as your grandchild can sit unaided she can have a high chair and sit at the table with the family. Help by putting lots of newspaper on the floor to catch the debris—and not worrying about the mess. Eating with the family will encourage your grandchild to try a wider range of foods. Babies like to copy and will often want some of what you're eating. When your grandchild grabs food off your plate, that's a sure sign she's ready for self-feeding.

> *" Be fairly easygoing about table manners with your grandchild and keep mealtimes relaxed "*

Mealtimes

Everyone wants mealtimes to be enjoyable so stay calm, no matter what happens. If your grandchild refuses food, it's easy to get angry or tense. Try to be relaxed about this when you're with her and help her parents relax too. Kids soon learn to use food as a weapon if it becomes an emotional issue. If everyone stays cool, then mealtimes are less likely to become battlegrounds.

The connections between food and love can be very close, and arguments about food and eating can be associated with tensions over other issues. In such cases, food and eating behavior—for example, refusal to eat—can become a weapon that a child uses either to get attention or to express anger or distress. It's best, therefore, to be fairly easygoing about table etiquette with your grandchild and keep mealtimes as relaxed as possible. When she's at your house, insist only on the aspects of table manners that you consider essential; refinements can come later. You can introduce "soft" rules fairly early, such as:

- We sit down on chairs to eat
- We don't eat while we run around
- We do as well as we can (no need to eat everything)
- We eat vegetables first.

My suggestions for meals for grandchildren 6–18 months

Vegetables

- When your grandchild is very young, make your own puréed vegetables and freeze it in ice cube trays for when you have her at your home
- Keep fresh veggies your grandchild can handle in the fridge—for example, cucumber sticks, tomato wedges, peas, corn, and carrot sticks
- A supply of frozen broccoli, string beans, and so on allows you to start any meal with lightly cooked veg.
- Try hummus and other dips made from different kinds of beans
- All my grandchildren have loved good old-fashioned thick vegetable soup—with a few lumps.

Fruit

- Lots of fresh berries served right on the high chair table
- As many seasonal fruits, such as mangoes, as you can find, served in slices. Try passion fruit and kiwi, or even papaya
- Get in year-round fruits such as apples, pears, oranges, tangerines, clementines, and bananas, cut into slices or wedges.

Protein

- Cottage cheese on the high chair
- Little slivers of skinless chicken for your grandchild to eat herself

- Morsels of roast lamb, beef, and turkey as above
- Salmon in small pieces as above
- Remove the bread crumbs from fish sticks
- Tofu—great for a first food
- Eggs—scrambled at first, then boiled later.

Good carbs (although avoid gluten for the first 6 months)

- Oatmeal
- Whole-grain cereals
- Whole-wheat bread slices
- Pasta
- Ravioli
- Gnocchi
- Brown rice
- Couscous.

Foods to make yourself

- Your own tomato sauce kept in the freezer for pasta dishes
- Beef or chicken croquettes
- Chicken patties
- Veggie burgers
- Fish balls
- Fish cakes
- Homemade fish sticks
- Scrambled egg
- Broccoli omelette
- Cauliflower with cheese sauce
- Vegetable soup
- Pure-fruit ice pops
- Fruit purées to eat with yogurt.

Eating between meals is OK

The old rule when we were young was three meals a day and no snacking. Now toddler-style grazing is known to be a perfectly healthy way of eating. It can be disconcerting for a grandparent, though, when a 12–15-month-old eating three good meals a day turns into an 18-month-old toddler who can't seem to eat a single decent meal and wants to subsist on snacks alone.

Relax!

Think back and you'll remember that toddlers need less food than a baby does in the first year because they aren't growing as fast. Your grandchild knows what she wants so there's no need to force food on her, otherwise mealtimes will become battlefields.

Healthy snacks

You might find your daughter puts healthy snacks (such as fruit, raisins, dried apricots, dates, cherry tomatoes, pieces of toast) around the kitchen at your grandchild's level so she can choose what she wants to eat, and when. This is a good way of feeding a child of this age so go along with it and don't worry.

The important thing is for your grandchild to have a balanced mix of healthy foods including protein (meat, fish, eggs, milk, cheese, and tofu), carbohydrates (bread, pasta, rice, potatoes, and breakfast cereals), and fruits and vegetables. What she eats is more important than when she eats, and she'll probably manage better with food in small quantities.

Let her choose
Offer your grandchild a selection of easy-to-hold snacks—she'll love to choose something for herself. Bread sticks, pieces of sugar-free cereal, and raisins are all suitable, but check with Mom.

Some reminders

Health advice changes as research improves our knowledge about food. It's a good idea to make sure you are up to date with current advice if you are going to be preparing meals for your grandchild.

There are a few foods everyone needs to be careful about. Toddlers should never be given undercooked or raw eggs, to avoid the risk of salmonella. But your toddler can safely eat cooked eggs regularly according to The American Heart Association. You can give your toddler as many as you'd like.

Whole or chopped nuts aren't advised for children under the age of five, to avoid the risk of choking, and it's best to avoid shark, swordfish, and marlin since they may contain relatively high levels of mercury, which could affect your grandchild's developing nervous system.

No salt should be added to a toddler's diet, and processed foods should be kept to a minimum because they contain excess salt, sugar, and fat. Where possible sugary foods and drinks should be avoided.

> **"** *Don't forget that a toddler or a child's portion is how much she can hold in the palm of her hand* **"**

Milk

The American Academy of Pediatrics advises that that babies at risk for obesity be weaned to 2 percent milk, rather than whole milk, from one year, until they are two years old. At two, all children should drink 1 percent (low-fat) milk. This switch to lower fat milk is thought to be especially good for girls. According to the Institute of Medicine it limits their exposure to pollutants that can be carried in animal fats.

How much to feed

Don't forget that a toddler or child's portion is how much she can hold in the palm of her hand. Babies and children are intimidated by piles of food so it's best to put too little on a plate rather than too much—she'll ask for more if she wants it. Once she stops eating, turns her head away when food is offered, or pushes her plate away, *don't persist*—that may cause overeating and you'll be creating a fussy eater. You're teaching her she can use food as a weapon to control you, which is an unhealthy lesson for any child.

What your grandchild likes

All my children and my grandchildren give me a pretty free hand with food and treats. Everyone knows that Granny occasionally breaks the rules, and that's OK. But, as a rule, don't go against your children's wishes on food—it's potentially incendiary! It is a good idea, though, to make sure you know the foods your grandchild likes so you can have them available when she comes to your house. It'll help her feel relaxed and at home.

Picky eaters

As you probably remember from your own children, in her second year a child will start to show likes and dislikes for certain foods. It's very common for children to go through phases of eating only one kind of food and refusing everything else. For example, she may go for a week only eating yogurt and fruit, then suddenly refuse yogurt and start eating nothing but cheese and mashed potatoes. Don't get upset about this, or try to pressure your daughter to make her eat certain foods. No one food is essential, and there's always a nutritious substitute for any food she refuses.

As long as a child is offered a wide variety of foods, she will have a balanced diet, and it's far better for her to eat something that she likes than nothing at all. The one thing everyone must watch out for is a toddler refusing to eat any food from a particular group—refusing any kind of fruit or vegetables, for example. If she does, her diet will become unbalanced. Perhaps you can help by thinking of ways of tempting her to eat fruit and vegetables, by cooking the food in a different way or presenting it imaginatively. It's hard for a busy mom to spend time making a pizza look like a smiley face, but you could offer to cook some fun dishes. You can even involve your grandchild in the cooking if she's old enough.

Let her help
If your grandchild is a picky eater, try getting her to help prepare the food—perhaps she could add the toppings to a homemade pizza? Few children will refuse food that they've made themselves.

Perhaps when you are taking care of your grandchild, you could encourage her to try some new foods. Offer new things when your grandchild is hungry, when she's more likely to take them. If she does, congratulate her. You might want to give "tasting points" for trying a new food, which add up to a star on a star chart, with prizes every now and then.

Treats and rewards

You might be surprised at how strict your son and daughter are about such things and it's important not to

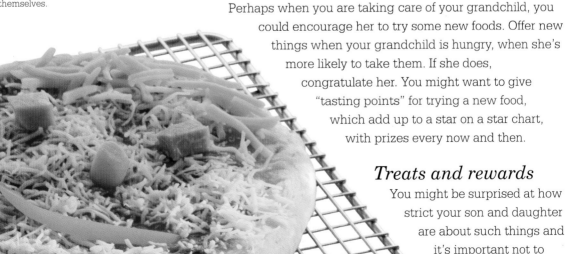

What if you eat meat and your son or daughter is a vegetarian?

What do you do if you enjoy lamb chops and your son or daughter wants your grandchild to grow up without meat of any kind? Medically I find this a tricky question, because there's no better-packed parcel of iron than red meat. Babies need iron in their food from six months on and sucking on a piece of red meat now and then will supply this.

In contrast, a baby would have to eat much larger volumes of fruit and vegetables to get similar amounts of iron, and their stomachs don't have the capacity. That being said, most vegetarians are well informed about nutritious foods and would substitute egg (with some iron) for meat.

If you find yourself in this situation you'd do best to become an enthusiastic supporter of your family's chosen diet. I would advise that you only offer a comment if your grandchild failed to thrive, grow, and develop well.

Trying it herself
It's good to encourage young children to make an attempt at brushing their own teeth. Then Mom or Grandma can finish up.

undermine their authority. Every grandparent loves to give their grandchildren little treats and rewards. But your daughter may feel that to give candy routinely as a reward goes against the family's approach to candy-eating in general. As always, stick to the rules of the house. Discuss this with your son and daughter and they will probably agree it's fine for you to give the occasional sweet treat, as long as you make it clear that it's a special one-time treat.

It's worth making an effort, though, to devise other forms of reward: a favorite yogurt flavor, a small toy, or a new box of crayons, or a specially extended bath time or bedtime story.

I don't believe in a total ban on candy or cookies, because this can encourage children to be secretive and dishonest. I do believe in rationing them, though, and this has worked with my own grandchildren. If you let your grandchild have a piece of candy after lunch and maybe a cookie after dinner, and then encourage her to brush her teeth afterward, you'll be encouraging self-control, good eating habits, and good oral hygiene.

"My grandchildren aren't disciplined"

Jack and Jessie worry that their daughter and son-in-law don't discipline their children enough. They say their grandchildren are allowed to get away with murder—they have no table manners and leave the table whenever they want. They don't do what they're told, talk back, and are rude sometimes. And they're not learning the value of things. They smash their toys to pieces rather than play with them. Jack and Jessie have told their daughter she should be firmer, but she just shrugs.

only then in public, not at home where there are so many distractions. Rudeness, though, is something else. Children need to learn from their parents how to conduct themselves well, but if parents don't correct their children there's not a lot grandparents can do, except try to teach by example.

I think grandmas have to be as relaxed as possible about how their grandchildren are being brought up. If not, the results can be disastrous. In one family I know the husband's parents were very critical and kept telling their daughter-in-law to do

I'd like Jack and Jessie to look for ways to praise their daughter and her family instead of nagging. They'll find there are plenty, and relations between them will improve

Every grandma and grandpa in the world has sometimes had the same thoughts as Jack and Jessie. It's traditional for the older generation to criticize the younger generation and think they're going to the dogs. But they aren't; they just do things differently than us and they think things we thought important aren't important at all.

As it happens, I have a relaxed approach to table manners. I don't think any child should be expected to sit still through a whole meal until they're four or five, and

things differently. They showed their disapproval of her all the time. One day she snapped and had a terrible row with her father-in-law and those grandparents have not seen their grandchildren since. I couldn't bear that to happen to me and I'm sure Jack and Jessie feel the same way.

I suggest that Jack and Jessie look for ways to praise their daughter and her family instead of nagging and worrying. They'll find there are plenty of opportunities to do so, and relations should quickly improve.

4 *Everyday Care*

Bathing your grandchild and changing her diapers are great ways to help out with her care. And how about learning baby massage?

Bathing your grandchild

Very young babies don't get dirty, so they don't need frequent bathing—but bath time does provide a perfect opportunity for cuddling and playing that infants come to relish. In the first week after birth, when your daughter will be very tired, you're the perfect helper to get this routine established.

Watch and listen

You'll know what to do, of course, but it's best to watch the baby's parents, see what they do, and follow their instructions. And as with many other aspects of your grandchild's care, you'll find that some things have changed. For example, many parents don't use any type of soap or bubble bath—they prefer to wash young babies with water alone. Also moms don't use talcum powder any more, since we now know it can be inhaled by babies.

Follow the nurse Your daughter's nurse will probably show her the best methods of bathing a new baby. It's best to follow these yourself, and not try to give your daughter conflicting advice.

First baths

Some new parents can be nervous about bathing their tiny baby at first so your experience and confidence can be very welcome. You can reassure your son and daughter that a baby is quite resilient, if he's handled gently but firmly, and encourage them to be as confident as possible.

Sponge baths

This—as I'm sure you will remember—is a short cut to cleaning a baby thoroughly by washing his face, hands, and diaper area, without undressing him completely. Most days it could be part of your grandchild's routine, giving him a bath only every two or three days, and your help will probably be welcomed. Here's what I do with my grandchildren.

- Undress the baby on a changing mat or towel. Leave his undershirt on or wrap him in a towel. Gently wipe his face, ears, and neck folds with a cotton pad moistened in warm water. Pat him dry.
- Carefully wipe his eyes from the inner corner outward by taking two more clean pieces of cotton pads and moistening them with cooled water. Be sure to use separate pieces of cotton pads for each stroke (to avoid the risk of cross infection).
- Take off his diaper and clean away any mess, then wipe with cotton pad moistened in warm water. Pay particular attention to the folds in his thighs. Then wash the genital area and pat dry. Apply a smear of emoilent cream, then put on a fresh diaper and clean clothes.

Make sure you have everything you need on hand:
- Cotton pads
- Cooled water for washing the eyes
- Bowl of warm water for washing the face and body
- Soft towels for wrapping and drying
- Diaper-changing equipment
- Clean clothes.

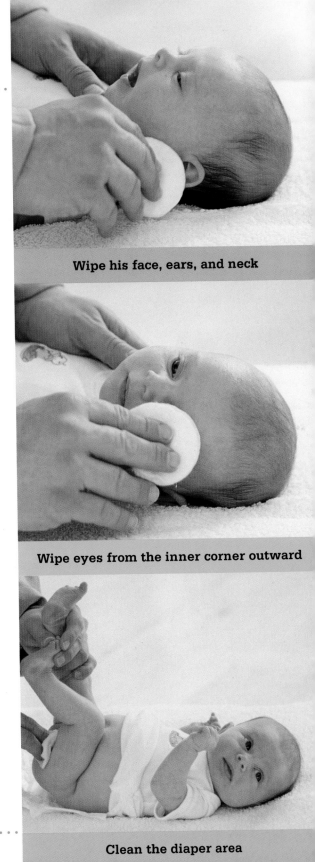

Wipe his face, ears, and neck

Wipe eyes from the inner corner outward

Clean the diaper area

Bath-time safety for both of you

Keeping your baby grandchild safe at bath time will be your greatest concern, but you also need to think about your own safety. You're out of practice and you might not be as strong as when you had young children yourself. You'll need to be careful not to strain yourself or hurt your back.

- Wash or bath your grandchild in a room that is warm and draft free. You can bath a baby anywhere—it doesn't have to be the bathroom and it doesn't have to be in a bath either. Use a bucket to carry the water to fill a large bowl or baby bath.
- Reserve a sponge and washcloth strictly for the baby's use and wash them frequently.
- Don't poke around inside a baby's ears with a cotton swab, since you could easily damage his delicate eardrums. Only remove ear wax that is visible at the opening.

" *Splash your grandchild's body gently to help her learn to enjoy, and be unafraid of, water* "

My bath-time solutions

When my grandchildren were tiny my favorite way of giving a bath was to get in the bath with them. It's a wonderful opportunity for bonding and we both felt safe and secure. Otherwise, I would kneel on the floor next to the bath, instead of leaning over and straining my back.

- When you take a bath with your grandchild, lay him on your chest half in and half out of the water. Smile and talk to him all the time as you clean him.
- Allow plenty of time; a bath isn't much fun for either of you if you have to rush. Remember, sharing a bath with a baby can also be a good and enjoyable way for you to wind down at the end of a busy day.

As your grandchild gets older

When your grandchild is four or five months old and has good head control, he might enjoy the big bath. Once he's gotten used to it, he'll appreciate the extra room to play in the water. As you'll remember, the same principles apply as when bathing a newborn—keep your grandchild warm before and after the bath, don't overfill the bath, and check that the water isn't too hot.

Do you remember…?
Bath-time routine for a young baby

I bring everything I'm going to need into the bathroom before bath time. I spread a big towel on the floor and put creams, diaper, clothes, and so on next to it. Then I can just lift my grandchild out of the bath, pop him on the towel, and wrap him up.

- Fill the bath 2–3 in (5–8 cm) deep, putting cold water in first. Test the temperature with your elbow or wrist; it should feel warm, not hot.
- Undress the baby down to his undershirt and wash his face and neck. Wrap him firmly in a towel. Holding him in a football carry under one arm and supporting his head with that hand, lean over the bath and gently wash and rinse his hair with water from the bath. Pat his hair dry with a towel.
- Leave a dry towel ready for after the bath. Remove the towel he's wrapped in, take off the diaper, and lift the baby into the bath, supporting his head and shoulders firmly with one hand, and his bottom and legs with your other hand.
- Holding the baby in the bath and supporting his head with one arm, gently wash his body with your free hand and encourage him to kick and splash in the water.
- To get the baby out of the bath, raise his head and shoulders with one hand and slide your free hand under his bottom as before, then lift him on to the dry towel. Wrap him up immediately so he doesn't get cold. Pat him dry all over, paying particular attention to the folds of his neck, bottom, and thighs as well as under his arms, then put on his diaper and dress him.
- Have all your equipment on the floor beside the bath and change the baby there. It's safer than carrying a wet slippery baby to a chair.

What you'll need:

- Baby bath
- Two towels
- Skin cream, if desired
- Cotton pads for face, eyes, and diaper area
- Cooled water for washing the eyes
- Diaper changing equipment
- Clean change of clothes.

Moving to the big bath

You will probably remember from your own children that the transition from the baby bath to the big bath can cause a few babies distress, although most love it. It's a good idea to begin by putting the baby bath into the big bath and firmly supporting him for the first few times, so that the change is gradual and less frightening for him. Once your grandchild gets used to it and can sit up in the bath by himself, he'll begin to look forward to it as part of his routine, and enjoy bath-time games and water play.

You'll find bath time can become a riotous affair with lots of shouts and splashing, and the problems may come when you want to get him out rather than getting him in! Bath time can become an enjoyable part of your grandchild's bedtime routine, so that it acts as a clear signal to him that the day is over.

When my grandchildren started to go in the big bath by themselves, I asked my daughter if I could have a chair or stool in the bathroom. That way I could sit and watch my grandchildren enjoy their bath without having to bend or stoop. When lifting a grandchild out of the bath, I make sure I'm standing steadily, so I take the strain with my legs, not my back.

And once the bath is over, I find that giving my grandchildren a hug in a lovely warm towel is a comforting end to bath time that they all enjoy.

Make sure you have everything you need on hand:
- Sponge or washcloth
- Baby bath treatment solution or an emollient bath oil in the bath water to moisturize your grandchild's skin
- Baby shampoo and conditioner
- Face shield to protect his eyes from shampoo
- Towel with a hood to keep his head warm—there are lots of great choices
- Diaper and night clothes.

Safety first

When you use the big bath, don't forget that a baby could drown in just a few inches of water. The following precautions make good sense:
- Put a nonslip mat in the bath.
- Never leave your grandchild alone in the bath, even when he can sit up.
- Turn the faucets off tightly before putting your grandchild in the bath. Never add more hot water while he is in the bath.
- Cover the faucets with a washcloth so he doesn't scald or hurt himself on them.

Hair washing

You will remember that even if a baby loves his bath, he may hate having water poured on his head or over his face, so hair washing can be a problem. Reassure your daughter that this is common and she shouldn't worry. If you try to force children to have their hair washed when they are upset, you run the risk of them rejecting the bath entirely. It's better to forget hair washing for a few weeks and just sponge his hair clean in the meantime. If a baby starts to associate hair washing with bath time, he may start to make a fuss about baths as well.

With my own grandchildren, their parents started getting them used to having water on their faces and heads from an early age—it's important for swimming too. They play games that involve bobbing their heads in and out of the water and dripping tiny amounts over the head from time to time, and the children have never had a problem with getting water on their faces. They don't even mind it in their eyes.

If your grandchild likes water and doesn't mind it on his face, you can use the bath shower attachment or a cup to rinse his hair and make a game of it. But even the mildest baby shampoo will sting your grandchild's eyes a little, so it's advisable to use a face shield to keep the soap and water out of his eyes until he's old enough to keep them shut or to hold his head back for you. Dry his hair with a towel and brush it gently with a soft brush. Once your grandchild has enough hair you might like to get him some baby conditioner to help make combing and brushing painless.

Getting a baby used to water
Gentle sponging is a good option for babies who hate having their hair washed. It's best, though, to get him used to having water on his face as early as possible.

Bath time with Dad

Why not encourage your son to deal with bath time by helping him at first? Your grandchild will grow to love his special time with Dad so encourage this bonding by supporting your son and giving him confidence. The more he baths the baby, the less nervous he will be of handling the slippery little body, and it's a good way of sharing the care.

Baby massage

After a bath or at a diaper change is an ideal time to massage your grandchild. Massage is a lovely thing for a grandparent to do and it can have all the benefits for a baby that it has for an adult: it's soothing, it calms a fretful baby, and it's a marvelous way of showing love.

A regular routine

If you massage your grandchild regularly she will learn to recognize the routine and will show pleasure as you begin. You can continue to massage your grandchild as she gets older; a massage is often the ideal way to calm an excited toddler.

Provide a relaxed atmosphere before you start. Choose a time when you're not likely to be disturbed, and turn off the telephone. Make sure the room is nice and warm, put on some calming music, and lay your grandchild on a warm towel or sheepskin, or on your lap.

Work from her head down, using light, even strokes, and ensure that both sides of her body are massaged symmetrically. Make eye contact with your grandchild throughout the massage and talk quietly, gently, and lovingly to her.

"Make eye contact with your grandchild throughout the massage and talk quietly, gently, and lovingly to her—it's a marvelous way of showing your love"

Babies love being touched. In fact, research has shown that they would rather be stroked than fed, so massage will be very beneficial. It can also sometimes ease minor digestive upsets, such as gas, which may make a baby fretful.

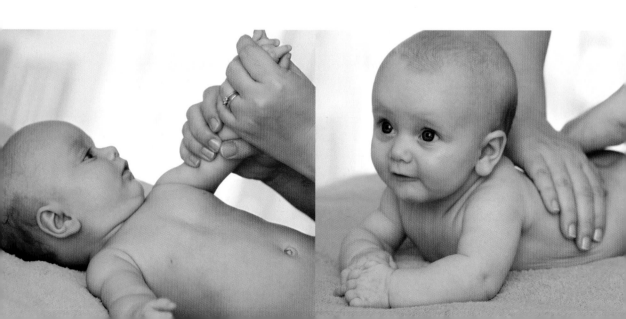

Giving your grandchild a massage

Make sure your hands are warm and use a good fragrance-free baby lotion. Don't use aromatherapy oils or any nut-based oil, such as almond oil. Stop massaging if your grandchild seems upset or not to be enjoying the massage.

Head

Start off by lightly massaging the crown of her head using a circular motion, then stroke down the sides of her face. Gently massage her forehead, working from the center out and moving over the eyebrows and cheeks to finish around her ears.

Neck and shoulders

Gently massage your grandchild's neck from her ears down to her shoulders and from her chin to her chest. Then carefully stroke her shoulders, working from her neck outward.

Arms

Stroke right down her arms to her fingertips. Using your fingers and thumb, gently squeeze all along her arm, starting at the top and working down toward her wrist and hand.

Chest and abdomen

Gently stroke down your grandchild's chest, following the delicate curves of her ribs. Then start to gently rub her abdomen in a circular motion, working outward from the navel.

Legs

Now you can massage her legs, working from her thighs down to her knees. Stroke down the shins, and move around to her calves and ankles. Gently squeeze all the way down.

Feet and toes

Rub her ankles and feet, stroking from heel to toe, and then concentrate on each toe individually. End with some strong, light strokes running the whole length of the front of your grandchild's body.

Learning massage
Baby massage is a wonderful way of bonding with your grandchild. You might find it comes naturally to you, but if not, look for baby massage classes at mothering groups.

Back

Once you have massaged your grandchild on her front, turn her over and work on her back. Massage from her shoulders downward and continue to talk quietly and gently to her as you do so. She'll be feeling very relaxed by this stage in the process and you probably will be too!

Benefits for grandparents

Massage is a delightful and valuable way of interacting with your grandchild and has advantages for you as well. It's easy to learn and a pleasure to do.

- If you're anxious, massage will help you to get used to handling your new grandchild.
- Massage is an ideal way to soothe an unsettled baby and can also help calm your nerves with its relaxing effects.
- You will find that massaging your baby's soft, smooth skin is a lovely experience for you as well as her.

Benefits for the baby

Being touched is an essential part of the bonding process that helps young creatures to thrive. Massage feels nice to a baby, just as it does to you, and the baby knows it is an expression of love.

- Your grandchild can only gain from the pleasures and sensations of a loving massage from you.
- Your grandchild loves being with you and the intimate contact of massage enhances this. She will recognize it as a clear sign of your love.
- If she's unsettled, your grandchild will be calmed by the soothing strokes of your hands, which will make her feel secure and relieve anxiety.
- As you massage, you're increasing your grandchild's awareness of the different parts of her body.
- Massaging your grandchild's skin is best, but if she doesn't like being undressed, dress her in a light cotton onesie, through which you can easily feel her body.

Hands and feet
It's a good idea to pay particular attention to your grandchild's hands and feet as you massage, readying them for grasping and standing.

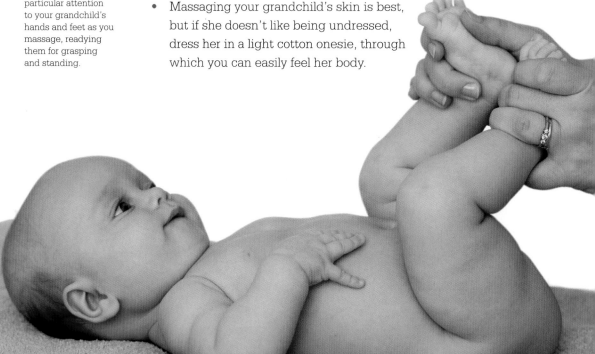

Your grandchild's diapers

Diapers—there's certainly plenty of choice nowadays, and designs that would only have been fantasy in my time. Many parents opt for disposables because they're so convenient. But others worry about the expense of disposables—and their environmental costs. They prefer reusable cloth diapers. Go along with whichever type of diaper your children choose.

Disposables or reusable?

You may be bewildered by the range available and the debate on the pros and cons of the different types. Disposables have many advantages—simple to put on, easy to get rid of, and convenient to carry around. Some are shaped to fit boys or girls. Boys tend to wet the front of diapers so boys' disposables have extra padding in the front. Girls tend to wet at the back of diapers more, and this is accounted for in the design of girl's disposables.

> **"** *There's a bewildering range of diapers available today, both disposable and reusable types* **"**

If your daughter opts for reusable diapers, you'll find there are huge improvements to the traditional terry-cloth square that required safety pins and which we tirelessly cleaned, washed, and sterilized. The latest cloth diapers are shaped like disposables so they fit around the baby without being folded. They fasten with Velcro tabs or snaps, so no need for pins. Some come with a built-in plastic outer layer; others need to be worn with plastic pants.

Unless your family uses a diaper laundry service, reusable cloth diapers are more trouble, since they have to be washed and dried. Disposable diapers are more expensive, even taking into account the hidden costs of washing and drying reusables. There's been much discussion about the adverse impact on the environment of disposable diapers both in their manufacture and disposal; reusable cloth diapers are probably more ecologically sound in the long run. However, if your grandchild does generally wear reusable diapers it's probably a good idea for you to have a pack of disposables at your own house for when you are taking care of him there.

Do you remember…?

You might think that you've forgotten all about how to change a diaper—particularly if faced with an unfamiliar design of diaper—but don't worry, it will all come back to you. You'll be whisking diapers off and popping new ones on with confidence in no time.

- Always do a diaper change on a firm, flat surface covered with a changing mat or towel.
- Protect your back by using a changing table of the correct height, or kneel beside the bed.
- Never leave a baby alone on the changing mat if it's on a surface above floor level. Even a newborn baby can wiggle off a mat, particularly if he's upset or angry, so make a habit of collecting all the equipment you need before you start.
- Dispose of feces in the toilet if possible; but don't flush disposable diapers or diaper liners down the toilet.
- Dispose of dirty diapers in diaper sacks, preferably placing them in a covered receptacle. There are now baby wipes that can be flushed down the toilet.
- Put reusable diapers in a diaper bin or bucket, depending on what system your daughter is using.

Baby wipes

You may or may not have had baby wipes when you were bringing up your children but you'll find there's a huge variety of wipes now, and they're an essential item by the changing mat, in the bathroom, kitchen, and baby bag. Never go out without them—they'll even remove drool, spit-up, and food stains from clothes.

Those for babies are very gentle. Some moisturize as well as clean and they leave the skin nice and soft. It's best not to use wipes on a newborn baby's skin, since it's fragile and easily broken. We know that friction in the diaper area predisposes a baby to diaper rash, so it's best to use water and cotton balls.

Nowadays there are even water-soluble wipes that can safely go in the toilet as long as you flush them separately. There are also biodegradable wipes that can go in a compost container.

Cleaning girls

Remember how you always clean a baby girl's diaper area from front to back to avoid spreading bacteria from the anus to the vagina? Don't clean inside the labia; just rinse away feces gently with damp cotton pads.

Cleaning boys

Remember how you cover a baby boy's penis with a tissue as you take off his diaper? Clean around his penis and scrotum with baby lotion. Don't try to pull back the foreskin, since it won't move until your grandson is much older. Always wipe the anus from front to back.

And just in case you've forgotten the routine...

Here's what you do. Follow this routine each time you change your grandchild's diaper and you can't go wrong.

Remove the dirty diaper and clean your grandchild carefully. Make sure all creases are clean and dry if you use water to clean. Slide the clean diaper under your grandchild, lifting his buttocks gently into position.

Dot on protective diaper cream to the diaper area at each changing to prevent diaper rash, and smooth it in gently.

Using both hands, bring the front of the diaper up between your grandchild's legs, as high as it will go. Tuck in the corners securely around his waist, ready for fastening.

Holding the diaper in place with one hand, attach the adhesive tabs firmly on to the flap of the diaper.

Make sure you have:
- Changing mat
- Baby wipes
- Diaper
- Bowl of warm water or baby lotion
- Cotton pads
- Diaper cream
- Diaper bags
- Container with lid.

Dot on some protective cream

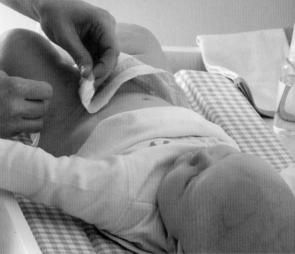

Fasten the tab on one side

Then the other—all done

Skin care for your grandchild

I am a dermatologist, so my children have always asked my advice on skin care for their babies. Baby skin, like adult skin, needs moisture, so I believe that a good baby moisturizing cream should be applied lavishly all over a baby's body every day up to the age of two.

The way to good skin

In our family we call this "creaming up" and it's become part of the routine for all my grandchildren. A perfect time to moisturize is after bathing and, at night, it could be part of a baby massage before bed. It's something I love to do for my grandchildren. Simple is best when choosing a cream. Avoid those with a long list of ingredients or that contain lanolin or paraffin wax, which can cause allergies.

This routine on its own will keep itchy dry skin at bay. But the second precaution is to keep a baby's skin free of water at the first sign of dryness or roughness because, paradoxically, water on the skin dries it out.

Soap on a baby's skin is a no-no. Soap dries out the skin, making it vulnerable to soreness and itchiness. I'm an advocate instead of an cream dissolved in bath water, which will cleanse the skin but moisturize it at the same time. Just notice how your grandchild's skin glows and how soft it feels afterward.

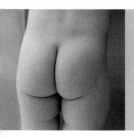

> **"** *Massaging in some cream to soothe their skin is part of the routine for all my grandchildren* **"**

Diaper rash

Diaper rash affects the area normally covered by a baby's diaper, and can happen whether the diapers are cloth or disposable. It bothers moms and grandmas, but it's preventable if you change the baby promptly, particularly after a bowel movement or when you get a whiff of a dirty diaper.

We used to think that the ammonia in urine was the culprit but now we know enzymes in feces break down the surface of the skin, which can go on to ulcerate. Diaper rash is encouraged in an alkaline environment, and because stools of bottle-fed babies are alkaline—unlike those of breast-fed babies, which are acidic—bottle-fed babies are more likely to suffer from diaper rash than breast-fed babies. That's another reason to encourage breast-feeding.

Staying smooth

The key is to keep your grandchild's skin dry and well aired. If he does get diaper rash your daughter may decide to use disposable rather than non-disposable diapers, until the skin is clear.

Always remove a smelly diaper immediately.

Cleanse the skin thoroughly with baby wipes.

Don't wash a baby's bottom with soap and water, since they both dry out the skin. Use lotion or wipes instead.

Start using a diaper cream at the first sign of broken skin.

Never leave a baby lying in a wet diaper.

Leave your grandchild's bottom open to the air whenever you can.

Do you remember...?

Here are some reminders of other causes of rash in the diaper area. Signs to look out for include redness over the diaper area or around the genitals.

Inadequate drying

A form of mild diaper rash can be the result of drying baby skin inadequately after bathing. Then the rash is usually confined to skin creases at the tops of the thighs.

Allergy

If a rash covers most of the diaper area, and the baby wears cloth diapers, the rash may be due to an allergic reaction to chemicals in the laundry detergent used. In this case, the skin creases are free of rash.

Baby eczema

Another kind of rash in the diaper area may be a sign of seborrheic eczema and treatment from the doctor will be needed.

Thrush (yeast)

A rash that starts around the anus and moves over the buttocks and on to the thighs may not be diaper rash but a thrush infection. A doctor can spot the difference.

Dressing your grandchild

Everyone loves dressing a baby, and you and all the family will all want to buy clothes for your grandchild as soon as he's born. You're bound to take great pride in your grandchild's appearance, and might want to buy some dressy clothes for special occasions, but there's no need to spend a lot of money—as you know, small babies grow out of clothes very quickly.

Comfort is key

You will find that styles have changed a lot since your day and there are even ranges from top designers for young children. As far as your grandchild is concerned, though, anything goes as long as it's soft and comfortable to wear, and can be put on and taken off really easily.

All young babies spit-up and drool on their clothes, and there are bound to be accidents and leaks from diapers. Your daughter will appreciate being given machine-washable, color-fast clothing as much as possible. Avoid white —it quickly gets dirty, and frequent washing makes it drab. Look for soft and comfortable clothes with no hard seams or rough stitching. Terry cloth, cotton, or pure wool clothes will feel nice to a baby's skin.

"As far as your grandchild is concerned, anything goes as long as it's soft and comfortable and can be put on and taken off really easily"

Things to remember

Look out for the modern fabrics that have emerged since our day—fabrics that wick moisture away, keeping the skin dry and free to breathe. And look for organic cotton if you're eco-minded. Clothes should always be nonflammable, and avoid open-weave wraps and cardigans—you'll remember how a baby's fingers can easily get caught in the holes. Check the fastenings, too: snaps at the crotch allow easy access to the diaper area, and snaps at the neck mean he won't grow out of something just because his head is too big for the neck opening.

You will remember how babies hate having their faces covered, so look for wide envelope necks or clothes that fasten down the front. And front-fastening clothes also allow you to dress him without having to turn him over, which will make dressing more comfortable for him and easier for you.

Measurements

Make a note of your grandchild's measurements and keep them with you when you're shopping. Babies of the same age vary a great deal in size, so look at the height and weight given on the label rather than the age.

Do you remember…?

When you're out shopping for clothes for your grandchildren, remember that easy-fitting clothes will be most comfortable. Check cuffs, ankles, and necklines, where fastenings could cause discomfort.

- Always buy clothes that can be machine washed—they won't stay clean for long.
- Choose hats that are practical and look good. Choose one with ties or elastic and a wide brim for sun protection or for warmth in winter. Hats with tie-down ear flaps are cosy in winter.
- Strong primary colors look good on both sexes.
- A jean and T-shirt set is comfortable and looks smart. Look for jeans with snaps at the crotch so that you can get at your grandchild's diaper easily.
- Don't think tights are just for girls; babies lose socks and booties very easily, so tights are practical as well as warm.
- Tracksuits are very comfortable, and slip off easily to allow access to your grandchild's diaper.
- Avoid fluffy cardigans that can irritate a baby's skin.
- Unisex clothes are ideal for everyday wear for your granddaughter, but you might like to buy some more feminine clothes for special occasions.
- If in doubt, buy the larger size, since loose clothes are warmer and more comfortable than those that are too small. And he'll soon grow into them.

Wide-brimmed hats offer sun protection

Jeans are good for boys and girls

A pretty dress is fun for special days

Dressing himself

Clothes are one of the first ways your grandchild expresses his individuality. By the time your grandchild reaches preschool age he'll probably want to select his clothes each day. Parents and grandparents might not always agree with his choices but having a flexible attitude encourages his developing sense of identity and independence.

The desire to dress himself is a milestone of development, expressing first and foremost burgeoning independence, but also a maturing dexterity and the desire to imitate what adults do for him.

Of course, his first attempts are on the clumsy side and he misses the mark but this is where you can really help your grandson, because you have the time and patience to wait (and encourage) while he tries, tries, and tries again to get his shoes and undershirt on (or off). All that patience really builds his self-confidence and determination and hones his emerging skills.

The same independent spirit is reflected in your grandchild's desire to brush his own hair and brush his own teeth, both of which you can encourage before finishing off the job yourself.

Let him try
Getting his socks on may take your grandson a while, but don't be tempted to interfere. Let him do this for himself to encourage his self-confidence and independence. Praise his success.

Helping your grandchild control herself

I'm starting with bladder control since it seems to bother parents more, even though bowel control can precede it. I feel I should put my cards on the table. I really have no time for the idea of "potty training." As a concept it's outdated, and it's unkind if attempted on a baby who isn't ready for it. The age when a baby is ready to be dry varies from baby to baby. There's no hard and fast rule.

Laid-back approach

The normal timeline is very long, but the facts are these: a baby who isn't ready cannot be trained; a baby who is ready doesn't need training.

As you'll have gathered, I'm in favor of a soft, laid-back approach where the baby takes the lead. Most problems arise where parents are determined to get a baby dry too early. Over enthusiasm, forcing a baby to sit on the potty and perform, then using discipline to enforce a parent's wants can lead to unhappiness.

"I'm in favor of a soft, laid-back approach where the baby takes the lead. A baby who isn't ready cannot be trained; a baby who is ready doesn't need training"

Of course you're there to back up what your children want to do but the kind way is to let your grandchild go at her own pace. There's no way you or anyone else can speed her up. But you can slow her down by being too strict. The thing to remember is that a baby can barely hold urine for *one second* until she is 15 months old. So while she may alert you that urine is coming with a grunt or by pointing, she can't hold it long enough to wait for the potty.

From then on she gains holding power very slowly, say a minute a week. So patience is only kind.

Your kind of practical help

Regardless of what approach your children take you can still follow a humane tack when you're in charge. Here are some suggestions for gently getting your grandchild used to the potty:

- From about a year, start using the potty as a toy so your grandchild has no fear of it.
- When your grandchild signals she wants to urinate, act quickly.
- Keep potties in several rooms, not just the bathroom, to familiarize your grandchild with them and for rapid use.

> **"** *Let baby take the lead. Most problems arise when parents are determined to get a baby dry too early* **"**

- Make light of accidents and praise all success enthusiastically.
- When your grandchild is using the potty, sit close by and read or tell a story.
- Use pull-up night diapers until your grandchild is completely dry, to remove anxiety about wetting herself. Girls commonly want to use them up to the age of four and boys five or later. It's normal. Let your grandchild decide when she no longer needs them.
- Never compare your grandchild to your past experience or to another child. It's not fair and you can't know how fast or slowly she's developing.
- Staying dry at night is helped by keeping liquids at a minimum before bedtime.
- Around the age of two your grandchild may ask to be left alone, and will be very proud of managing the potty on her own.
- Insist on going on the potty before outings and going to bed.
- Place a potty near the bed so she can use it if she wakes at night.
- Keep a supply of pull-up diapers for when your grandchildren come to stay.

You know from experience not to expect more than this rough timetable suggests

I must stress that the ages given below are very rough guidelines, based on averages. And as I'm sure you know, no child is average and the spread of what is considered to be normal is extremely wide.

- 18 months—most girls are almost dry during the day—add six months for boys
- 2½ years—many girls are almost dry at night—boys, six months later
- 4 years—nine out of 10 children will be dry day and night
- It follows that one out of 10 children will still need a pull-up at night at the age of five and this is normal.

Your practiced eye—your relaxed style

Parents seem to get quite worked up about bowel control and here you can be the calm voice of reason and quietly protect your grandchild from an overzealous mom and dad. You'll remember that there is nothing to panic about and all children get there eventually.

Let her develop at her own pace

A very simple scenario will tell you how counterproductive it is to attempt to train a baby to do poop in her potty. Any child loves to be the center of attention. If you're in any way obsessive about obtaining a bowel movement when you expect it by insisting on potty-sitting, a child will quickly learn that she can always claim your attention by withholding. This is the first step you've taught her about manipulating you through using the potty. She learns very quickly that you'll make a fuss of her if she *doesn't* go. This isn't the way to encourage healthy bowel habit—it could lead to constipation.

Your children may have other ideas but this is how you can help when your grandchild is with you, when you're babysitting and when you're in charge. When you have the opportunity, the golden rule is for you to let your grandchild develop at her own pace and make it easy for her to do so.

You can help everyone in the family. Remember not to be tense about anything to do with your grandchildren using the potty or toilet. Any anxiety on the part of the grown-ups will quickly be picked up by the child, so it's important to keep the atmosphere relaxed and be very calm yourself.

Never criticize your daughter about her dealings with the potty—you certainly don't want tensions on this arising between the two of you. Follow her lead. If you do want to discuss things, do it out of the child's hearing.

Distractions
You can help to make sure that any time your grandchild spends on the potty is happy and relaxed. Try reading to her and she'll soon get so involved in the story that she'll forget she's on the potty.

What to expect

As before, this timetable is very approximate so don't worry if your grandchild doesn't conform, but you might find the suggestions for helping her useful.

15 to 18 months old

Your grandchild may automatically empty her bowels after eating, so casually put her on the potty after meals.

What you can do to help

- It's probably too soon for your grandchild to begin using her potty, but you can get her used to it by offering it as a seat while she looks at a book or plays with a toy.
- As soon as she can sit up on her own, you can put her on the potty for a few moments after meals.
- Never leave her longer than a few moments, and if she gets bored, lift her off.
- Say "Well done" if she has a bowel movement, and don't comment if she doesn't.

18 months to two years old

Your grandchild is happy and relaxed sitting on or playing with the potty.

What you can do to help

- Let her come into the bathroom with you, so she can imitate you when she's ready.
- Encourage her to feel happy and relaxed, with whatever she does with, or in, the potty.

Two to two-and-a-half years old

Your grandchild's desire to be clean and independent is very strong, so take your lead from her when offering her the potty.

What you can do to help

- Encourage her by praising her after a clean night, even though she still may be wet.
- Don't be too anxious about wanting her to stay clean. Wait for her signal or request.
- Give praise if she stays clean. Bowel control is often accomplished before bladder control, so it's important to discriminate between the two and praise each achievement when it happens.

Three to five years old

Your grandchild can now control and retain her stool so that she has time to get to the bathroom without an accident.

What you can do to help

- Most children are clean by five, but by no means all. Stay calm.
- Dress her in clothes that are easy for her to pull down when she has to use the toilet.

"I feel jealous of fellow grandparents"

Jane worries that the other set of grandparents in her family see more of her grandchildren than she and her husband do. She notices that they get to visit more often, and when her granddaughter let slip that the other grandparents went on vacation with the family last summer Jane felt jealous. Jane has looked forward to getting really close to her grandchildren for years and now feels that her daughter-in-law favors her own parents. Should Jane tell her how she feels?

These days, with complicated families due to divorce and remarriage, children can have several sets of grandparents. There are four sets in the family of one my stepdaughters and there's a hierarchy, of course. I come lowest of the four and I'm happy in that position. I consider myself privileged that my stepdaughter includes me at all. I treat her children the same as my own grandchildren and I feel that as they grow up, her children will see me as a loving grandma. I trust the children to make the choices, not the grown-ups.

> Perhaps Jane could talk to to her son and get his help?
> And she could suggest that all four grandparents meet for
> a meal so she can show that she doesn't hold a grudge

I think what Jane is describing happens the world over and there's nothing to be done about it. A daughter will always favor her own mother—unless she's exceptional. I do have an exceptional daughter-in-law who makes me feel very welcome and goes out of her way to include me. I think this is probably because I like her so much and I tell her often. I tell her I love her as though she is my own daughter and that I think she's a great mom. I go out of my way to praise how she's bringing up my grandkids.

I'd advise Jane to be careful about approching her daughter-in-law. After all, it's her mom she's talking about and they're obviously very close. It might be better to have a talk with her son instead and explain to him how she feels. If he can be an ally, he could subtly try to redress the balance between Jane and her daughter-in-law's parents. Perhaps Jane could suggest that the four grandparents meet up for a meal so that she can show everyone she doesn't hold a grudge.

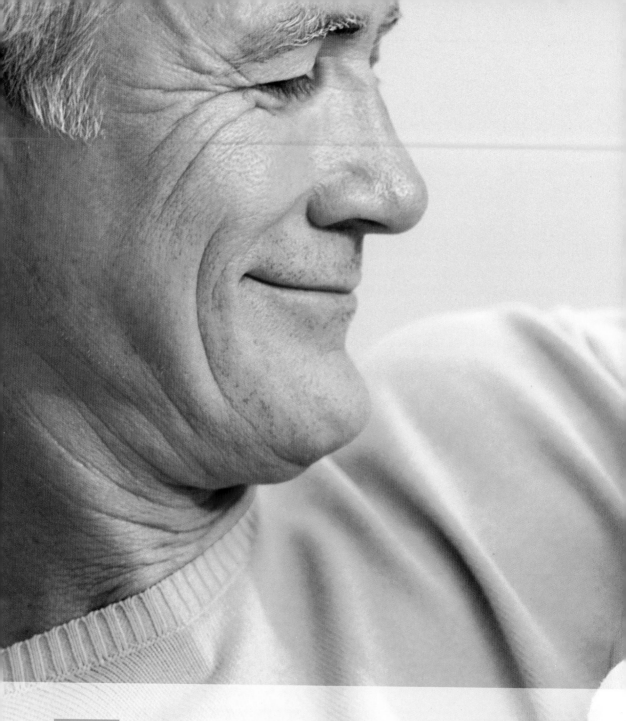

5 Comforting Your Grandchild

Loving grandparents can play a useful role in soothing young babies and helping to teach them ways of self-quieting.

"*Every time a baby is touched and caressed, that touch activates growth hormones, which encourage healthy development*"

Babies need comforting

Most first-time parents are shocked when they realize how much a baby cries, and it can worry and upset them. As grandparents, we're able to reassure our children because we can take the long view and know that crying usually settles down after the first few weeks or months.

Should babies be left to cry?

You may, though, find yourself at odds with your children when it comes to settling down and comforting a crying baby, since there are several modern schools of thought. It's good to know about these but, as always, the golden rule of good grandparenting is to back up your children in their chosen approach.

One of the most popular fashions of the moment for training a baby to sleep is a technique known as controlled crying. This means the baby is left to cry for long periods, with the hope that in the end he will stop crying and eventually learn to put himself to sleep. I have to take a stand here. I find the idea of letting a baby cry for long periods until he falls asleep exhausted abhorrent—abhorrent at the level of human kindness and abhorrent for what this stress does to a baby's developing brain (see page 103).

You'll probably meet parents who swear by this method and your children may want to use it, so it's good to know what it's all about.

"There are several modern schools of thought on settling babies down, but the golden rule of grandparenting is to back up your children in their choices"

Controlled crying

Controlled crying is a way of training (not teaching) a baby to fall asleep on his own. The principle is that you leave the baby to cry for, say, five minutes, then return to check that he's all right. You don't go to the crib, don't pat, hold, or comfort him, but firmly tell himto go to sleep and you'll see him in the morning.

You then extend the interval by five minutes each time up to 15 minutes, but with a vigorously crying baby you can start with a 10-minute interval, extending to 20 minutes. Advocates claim that if the rule is properly applied a child should cry for little more than an hour.

It's claimed to be quick and easy, taking a maximum of seven to 10 days to work. But it can be grueling and emotionally exhausting, especially if the baby cries so much he vomits. It's usually used for babies between the ages of six months and three years. Adherents claim it does a child no psychological harm but the latest research disputes this, since during crying the baby's brain is bathed in stress hormones, which affect both brain growth and function.

Why I believe that controlled crying is harmful

Fortunately there is now robust scientific evidence to challenge the harshness of the controlled-crying brigade, and this is important to know about and understand. It goes as follows. Stress in infancy, caused by leaving a young baby to cry, is particularly painful because if ignored it results in high levels of stress hormones that dampen the formation of a healthy brain. A baby is born expecting to have stress managed for him—by his parents. The prefrontal cortex (the frontal lobes), the part of the brain which exerts control over emotions, is virtually nonexistent at birth.

Stress hormones will remain low if a parent, or another caring adult such as a grandparent, teaches a baby to trust by holding, stroking, feeding, nuzzling, reassuring, whispering, and laughing. However, since a baby's emotions are unstable, those stress hormones can shoot up if there's no caring adult alert to his emotional needs and prepared to calm him and comfort him when he's upset.

To put it as bluntly as Sue Gerhardt in her marvelous book *Why Love Matters*, a baby can't tune out his stress hormones, he needs a caring adult to switch them off for him. The simple truth is that your grandchild doesn't have the equipment, anatomical or physiological, to deal with distress, because the part of the brain that would help him cope doesn't come on board for another four to six months. That's why I think controlled crying is unfair.

The best kind of mother

I firmly believe that the best kind of mother is one who hugs her child when she feels the child needs a hug, who lifts her child when she thinks that her child wants to be picked up, and who puts him down when she thinks her baby is ready for sleep. The same mother will feed her baby when he's hungry (and not clock watch) and let him sleep when she senses he's tired. A grandparent can be a most valuable assistant here, helping to give a baby the intense love and reassurance he needs. A baby can't have too much.

Give him comfort
A baby's brain just hasn't developed enough for him to calm himself down. He needs an adult to comfort him when he's upset and switch off his stress hormones.

Hugs and reassurance

A baby's whole system is molded by how much early stress she has to contend with and how well her caregivers help her deal with it. I believe what a baby needs is the kind of parents—and grandparents—who help her recover her equilibrium. If you do this, the baby will learn to regulate her own stress hormones and her own emotions with them.

Babies need love

On the other hand, if she's left to contend with stress and no one helps her she'll release stress hormones at the smallest stressor. She'll be a baby who cries easily, remains upset despite comforting, and is inconsolable.

Not the least of the baby's organs to be affected is her brain. In their fascinating book *A General Theory of Love,* three psychiatrists, Professors Lewis, Amini, and Lannon, suggest that the bond of love, or the lack of it, affects a baby's brain forever. This is because insecurity in early life leads to changes in a baby's brain chemistry. The levels of mood-lifting chemicals such as serotonin and dopamine are lowered and imprinted into a baby's brain in the first few months of her life.

The professors believe that with the wrong kind of mothering (letting a baby cry for long periods) this alteration of brain chemistry becomes hardwired, unchangeable, and permanent, leading to timid, clingy children; neurotic, withdrawn teenagers; and adults vulnerable to anxiety and depression.

> **" *A grandparent can help give a baby that intense love and reassurance that she needs* "**

In stressful situations, the hardwiring floods the brain with the stress hormone cortisol rather than the calming hormones serotonin and dopamine. The body and brain are on alert, ready for fight or flight.

A responsive parent helps a baby to balance her emotions. A baby who's upset depends on her mother to be a reliable source of comfort because she can't soothe herself. After being soothed many times, a baby remembers the feeling of consolation, is able to tap into it herself, and so learns to quiet herself. She knows she's secure and so comes to know what security feels like.

Good experiences early on in life produce brains with more neural connections—more richly networked brains. With more connections, there's better brain performance and more flexibility to use particular areas of the brain. Between six and 12 months, in the tender care of a loving parent, there's a massive growth spurt in these connections in a baby's brain, just at the time when the pleasurable relationship with a baby is most intense.

Encourage positive experiences

A baby remembers and stores negative incidents, looks, and memories. A negative experience can trigger a chemical response just as a positive one can. Once stress hormones are set off they stop the flow of endorphins and dopamine and kill pleasurable feelings. Allan Schore, another researcher in this area, believes that looks, smiles, and comforting experiences actually help a baby's brain to grow. Schore suggests that these early positive and loving experiences are the most vital stimulus for the growth of the social, emotionally intelligent brain.

When a baby feels pleasure a chemical cascade of happiness flows through her. First a pleasure hormone called beta-endorphin is released into the circulation, and specifically into the prefrontal region of the brain. These natural opioids help brain cells to grow by controlling glucose and insulin. They also make a baby feel good.

> **"***All that cuddling, gentle words, and doting looks fire off the pleasure chemicals that help the social brain to grow* **"**

At the same time another hormone, dopamine, is released from the prefrontal cortex. This also enhances the use of glucose, helping new brain cells grow. If you want to know what this energizing and stimulating effect feels like, just imagine being rewarded for a job well done. All that cuddling, gentle words, and doting looks a baby receives fire off the pleasure chemicals that help the social brain to grow. Which parent or grandparent can resist that promise and not go to their crying baby?

The admirable developmental psychologist Mary Ainsworth has shown that every time parents and grandparents act on their natural instincts they're encouraging a happy, secure child. Every time a baby is touched and caressed, that touch activates growth hormones, encouraging healthy development.

"Good experiences early on in life produce brains with more neural connections—more richly networked brains"

Self-quieting

One of the greatest skills that an adult can teach a baby is the art of self-quieting. To do this for a baby is to set him off on his journey to independence and self-confidence. It's unfair to encourage him to depend on any adult in order to get him off to sleep. And you, as grandma, can help him master this skill.

Grandma's role

Not all babies will go down easily and quietly when taken from a stimulating environment to a tranquil one—after being nursed on a parent's lap before being put into the crib. At least half of babies require more than that and we should give time, effort, and love to help a baby learn to quiet himself so he can drop off to sleep on his own. I believe Grandma can have a very special role in helping babies learn self-quieting—you have the time and patience that parents may not be able to devote.

"All a baby needs to know is that someone is there, and your comforting presence may be enough to help him to self-quiet"

Even though a baby may be tired and want to go to sleep, he may need some physical contact in order to drop off. This is one of the reasons why I'm wholeheartedly against leaving babies to cry, because in doing so we're not providing them with the help they need in order to settle down. Physical contact doesn't mean that you lift the baby, cuddle with him, walk around the room with him on your shoulder—all he needs to know is that you're there, and your comforting presence may be enough to help him to self-quiet.

Once he's in the crib, simply pat him firmly and rhythmically. At the same time murmur a calming sssssssssssh noise and prolong the shush sound over a couple of pats. Most babies will stop crying when you do this because they can't concentrate on crying while you're firmly patting and shushing them. Keep the patting and shushing going until he stops crying, but don't stop—continue patting and shushing for several minutes after he stops crying.

If he doesn't quiet within a few minutes, lift him out and shush and pat him on your shoulder until he stops crying. Replace him in his crib and continue with firm patting and shushing for about 10 minutes after he stops crying. Even once he's quiet, don't stop. If he's still quiet after 10 minutes, you can gradually slow the patting down and quiet the shushing. But stay in the room with him for several minutes longer because it'll take a baby about 20 minutes to get into deep sleep. We don't want him to jerk awake before then and find that you're not there to comfort and calm him.

Giving a baby confidence

I believe that helping a baby to self-quiet with this sort of technique will mean that from four months onward he'll be in a strong position to quiet himself easily and quickly when put into his crib. You've given him the confidence to take care of himself. He has stored up good memories of what it feels like when he slips off into sleep feeling secure, and he can tap into these feelings when he's laid down in his crib.

The main thing that makes it difficult for a baby to love his crib and self-quiet is inconsistency. If, for instance, parents decide at the beginning that they're going to use the family bed when the baby is born there comes a point when he has to be moved into his own crib. This is a difficult transition for any baby to make because he's been brought up to expect his parents' presence in order to go off to sleep and to remain asleep. But now he's being deprived of that. Naturally he's upset and he may even feel abandoned. He may be too insecure to go back to sleep once he's in a crib. You can see that while co-sleeping may be convenient for parents, it doesn't help develop a baby's independent skills of going to sleep on his own. The result is that the all-important bond of trust, which is essential for him to grow into an independent, secure child, is broken.

A gentle hand
The physical contact a baby needs for reassurance and comfort may be just a gentle hand laid on his chest. This simple touch will soothe him and show him that someone is there.

I'm on the side of the baby on this and in any other situation where his trust in his caregivers may be eroded. One such would be letting him cry for longer and longer periods as is advocated in controlled crying—you'll eventually end up with a baby who no longer trusts you as his source of comfort and learns to depend on himself by default.

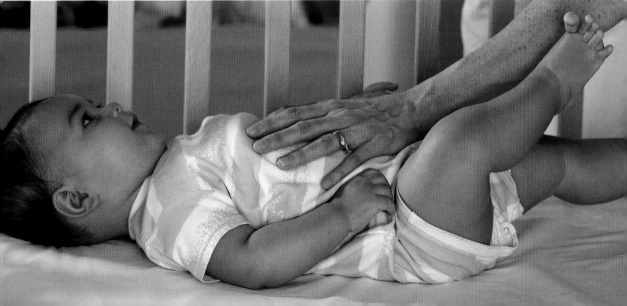

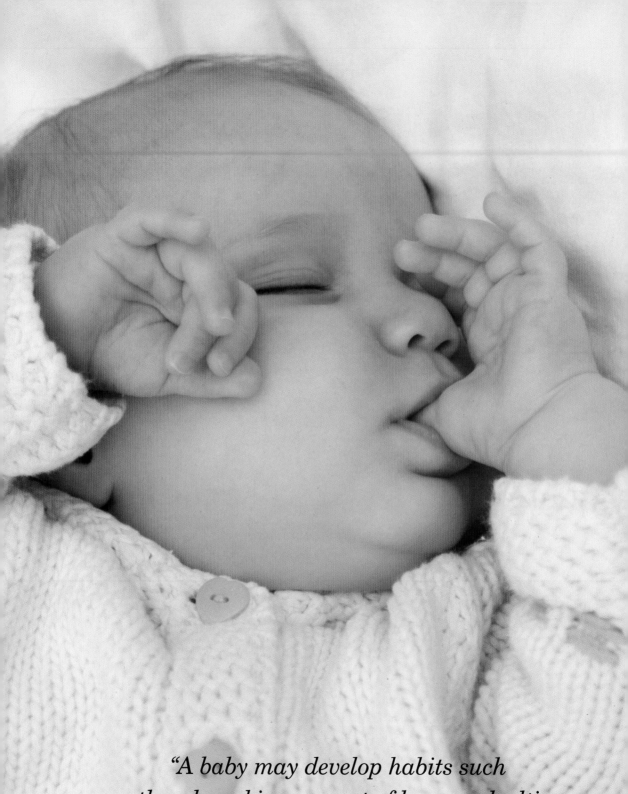

"A baby may develop habits such
as thumb sucking as part of her own bedtime
routine and her self-quieting ritual"

While it may help a baby in the short term, many babies who have been left to cry by themselves grow into chronically bad sleepers from that point on. Furthermore, robust research shows that these babies cry more as they get older. Some of them put up a terrible battle when it comes to bedtime, even becoming fearful of their own cribs, resulting in the baby's daytime schedule being turned upside down. To drop off out of exhaustion is no way at all for a baby to fall asleep.

Once a baby has become distrustful of his caregivers and dislikes his crib it can take a month or more of gentle bedtime teaching to overcome these problems. Better not to let them happen in the first place.

" Babies have a natural desire to suck so I see no harm in giving a baby a pacifier if he wants one "

Comfort aids

Up to the age of four or five months a baby's only source of self-comforting is to suck, which is why many babies, indeed all babies who are breast-fed, will quiet down as soon as they're put on the breast. Many times they want the comfort that comes from sucking more than the food.

Up to this age, and in order to satisfy their natural desire to suck, there's no harm in giving a baby a pacifier. Once a baby has found his fingers, however, it's a simple matter to help him put his finger in his mouth, replacing the pacifier. If, however, he continues to want a pacifier at night I see no reason to deprive him of it.

Being able to fall asleep on his own is so important that I believe a child should have as many comfort aids and comfort habits as possible. A baby may become attached to a comfort item—a soft doll, a small handkerchief, a torn piece of blanket, or a burp cloth—and he may also develop habits such as rocking, thumb sucking, or twisting his hair to create his own bedtime routine and self-quieting ritual. There's nothing wrong with any of these bedtime rituals. By using a comfort aid to help himself go to sleep, a baby is using his inner resources and learning to become self-reliant. Once he's self-reliant he'll give up these habits in his own time. So why resist them? It would be quite wrong to take them away from him or to try to break him of his comforting habits.

Tantrums and tears

You'll remember temper tantrums all too well and the frustrations of dealing with a screaming toddler. You'll also remember that this is normal behavior at this age and not be too fazed when your grandchild lets lose with a screaming fit in the supermarket. Because you've seen it all before, you're less likely to be alarmed by such antics than Mom or Dad, who may not have witnessed them before.

Dealing with tantrums

A young child does not have sufficient judgment to control her strength of will or the ability to express her frustrations, so she vents her anger. She may cry, throw herself on the ground, kick, and scream. Advice on how to deal with all this hasn't changed much since our day—as always, the most important thing is to stay calm, since any attention on your part will only prolong the attack. If your grandchild has a tantrum in public, take her away from too much attention without making a fuss.

If you're at home, the best thing to do is to leave the room, having made sure the child will be safe. Explain to your grandchild that, while you still love her very much, you have to leave the room because you are getting upset. Never confine her in another room because this denies her the option of coming back and saying sorry.

" *Toddlers cry very easily at what might seem to be minor upsets and you need to be patient to soothe their woes* **"**

Comforting toddlers and preschoolers

Children of this age cry very easily at what might seem to us to be minor upsets, such as a scraped knee, and you need to be patient to soothe their woes. Hugs are just not always enough. I have a four-stage plan for comforting, which nearly always works, and helps children learn how to handle their emotions and quiet themselves.

- Legitimize the reason for crying—if she's had a little bump, for example, sympathize and say that you know it must hurt. Don't try to make her be brave or scoff at her distress.

- Comfort her with a big hug and lots of soothing words to show that you understand how she's feeling.
- Distract the child from what has happened. Suggest a special game or a treat after lunch.
- Quickly move on to whatever you are going to do and the tears will soon be forgotten.

A magic band-aid

A band-aid can work wonders if a child has had a little mishap, even if the injury doesn't need it. The band-aid is a welcome distraction, especially if it is covered with cartoon figures.

When my children were young I always had some "magic cream" (mild antiseptic) on hand for minor bumps and scratches. They would respond immediately to the attention, so the cream worked wonders every time.

I want Mom

As children grow past babyhood it can sometimes become harder for anyone other than Mom or Dad to provide comfort when they are upset about something or afraid. You may find that your three-year old grandchild suddenly rejects your hugs and cries for her mom, but don't be upset. It's not personal—your grandchild is just recognizing that there is a hierarchy in her world and that her parents are at the top of it.

At this stage children are still very worried by separation from their parents and may be fearful that they will not come back. If you are babysitting, don't lie to your grandchild and say that Mommy will be back any minute if she's gone out for the whole evening. Instead, reassure her by explaining exactly what will happen step by step: that Grandma will give her a bath, read her a story, and put her to bed, and Mommy and Daddy will be there in the morning. I find that the more details you can give, and the more you confirm those details, the better. What I say to my grandchildren is, "Mommy and Daddy always come back."

Dethronement

A time when Grandma and Grandpa really come into their own is when a grandchild is dealing with the arrival of a new baby in the family. She may feel her position in her parents' affections is in danger and she may revert to baby behavior and tantrums in order to get more attention—she is feeling dethroned. As a grandma, you can give your grandchild the special attention and reassurance she seeks at this time. You can provide that extra love and rebuild her self-esteem and self-confidence with your good grandmaship and your ability to give the one-on-one devotion that she so badly needs.

Mom's cuddles
There's no doubt that Mom's loving cuddles and caresses can soothe nearly all a child's ills. But if Mom isn't around, Grandma or Grandpa can make a very good substitute.

"My grandson has Down syndrome"

Lynn's new grandchild has Down syndrome and she doesn't know how to come to terms with the situation. He's her first grandchild and she's dreamed about how she would watch him grow up and looked forward to doing things together. She says that he's a sweet little boy and smiles and gurgles a lot, but she just can't relate to him as she would if he were "normal." Lynn doesn't feel like a real grandmother and says that she is so unhappy she often cries herself to sleep. What can she do?

her grandson and I urge her to start right away. It would be such a shame to miss out on those wonderful early days.

A life is a life and a baby with Down syndrome has exactly the same right as any other child to the best life possible. That means being loved, cherished, cared for, and educated, and being as normal as possible. Children with Down syndrome have many winning ways; they're happy, do well in mainstream school with special attention and teaching, and some enjoy an independent life with a little help.

I'd urge Lynn to stop feeling sorry for herself and think of her grandson. Try to be his biggest fan, coach, and cheerleader and be proud of him and his achievements

My friend's daughter has a child with Down syndrome and getting to know him has been one of the greatest joys of my life. He's six now and goes to school. He's very bright and always cheerful. He loves music and we have sing-alongs together when he bangs a tambourine. I take him to the park with my grandchildren and they play very well together. He keeps up and he's great fun. The children all love him and see him as "normal." So I would say to Lynn that she could have a lovely future getting to know

This is my advice to Lynn: Why deprive yourself of so much happiness? Instead of crying and complaining, try to be your grandson's biggest fan, coach, and cheerleader. Step outside of your reluctance to be a real grandma to him and be proud of him and his achievements. He'll pay you back a thousand times. Start thinking about your grandson instead of yourself and find out as much as you can about how to help him. He needs you even more than if he were a "normal" baby.

6 *Sweet Dreams with Grandma and Grandp*

Be up to speed with the latest thinking about bedtime and sleep issues, but always let your children make their own decisions on what's best.

Babies and sleep

Getting a baby off to sleep can be one of those things that many new parents find difficult and become very anxious about. It's an area where Grandma can really help. You have the experience and the calm confidence to know what your grandchild needs and how to help him develop good sleep patterns.

Sleeping alone

Helping a baby learn to sleep alone is vital. Parents often think that a baby should automatically be happy to sleep alone when put into a silent room in his crib. As you will remember, this is rarely the case. And when you think about this, it makes perfect sense because, until birth, the baby has been inside his mother with her warmth and heartbeat for constant comfort.

"As a grandma, you have the experience and calm confidence to know what your grandchild needs and how to help him develop good sleep patterns"

A sound sleep
To sleep soundly, a baby needs to be warm, but not too warm, so don't overdo the blankets.

Being left alone is a big shock at first, which is why babies cry and fret to begin with and need to be taught that sleeping on their own is OK. I never advocate letting babies cry to get them used to this. Crying for long periods programs the brain to become easily distressed and inconsolable (see page 102)—and once in that state, a baby won't sleep. He needs to feel safe and loved; swaddling can help with this in the first few weeks, and so can stroking and talking in a low voice if he cries.

How Grandma can help

From the long perspective of grandmahood, my experience tells me that babies and children sleep better and longer if there are some well-chosen house rules about sleeping. All babies and children love ritual and routine—it makes them feel secure—and where there has been no routine before, bad habits can often be replaced with good ones simply by following some cues and rituals that will quickly become second nature (see pages 128–9). As a grandma, I'm able to give time to these rituals at the end of the day, when parents may be feeling rushed and stressed after a busy day.

Books abound on how best to get babies and children to sleep. And your own family will probably cull tips from many sources to arrive at their own way of doing things. You may be one of those sources, which will be gratifying, but you may also find some practices which are unfamiliar to you, even alien, but you must go along with them. I've learned to follow my children's house rules and I see my grandchildren skip happily into their bedrooms to go to sleep.

A few things to remember

Whatever techniques your children choose for getting the baby to sleep, always back them up. See yourself as an enthusiastic member of the team whose goal is to secure happy bedtimes for your grandchildren. You might find it helpful to keep the following in mind.

The more a baby sleeps, the more a baby sleeps

This means that a baby who naps regularly, morning and afternoon, when he's young will sleep well during the night too. A baby who's starved of his nap will probably be overly tired and upset and will also have difficulty getting to sleep at night.

Independent sleep fosters better sleep

A baby who can go to sleep on his own, and who can self-quiet and self-comfort, will automatically generate his own contented sleep, but he can't learn to do that on his own. It's the job of adults to help, encourage, and teach him how to get off to sleep in a kind and humane way.

Babies have to be *taught* to sleep on their own

A newborn baby probably sleeps in excess of 16 hours a day for the first few weeks and sleep seems a very natural thing for a baby to do. Even so, a baby still has to be helped and taught to sleep in a way that encourages him to sleep on his own in his crib, without being held, nursed, or cuddled in order to drop off.

The way a baby sleeps

I'm sure you will recall that during the first year a baby changes the way he sleeps, both in terms of the length of time he spends sleeping and when he sleeps, as he shifts from daytime to nighttime sleeping. But I'm going to run through the changes that happen during this first year to help you support your grandchild's parents if they are worrying about sleep problems.

The first few months

As you'll know, in the first three months a baby's sleeping pattern is fairly unpredictable and this is because a baby can't distinguish between night and day. Being awake is largely due to whether he's hungry or not.

> **❝** *Most babies can't sleep through the night until they are about 12lb (5.5kg). It's weight that's important at this stage, not age* **❞**

However, during the first three months it's possible to start teaching a baby about nighttime sleeping by making sure that the room is darkened whenever he's put down for sleeping. Once he understands nights are his main sleep time it could mean that daytime naps will drop from about three to four hours to two to three by the end of the third month. He'll be sleeping for longer periods at night and, by three months, possibly sleeping through the night—though remember that this depends more on his weight than anything else. Most babies can't sleep through the night until they are about 12lb (5.5kg). It's weight that's important at this stage, not age.

Six months and over

By the time a baby is six months, he'll need no more than about 14 hours' sleep a day. His sleep needs are driven by how quickly he's developing. Remember, it's from three to six months that parents can really influence and teach their baby to slip into a good sleep routine. By nine months he'll probably need a morning and afternoon nap and sleep for almost 12 hours unbroken at night.

When he's a toddler, the morning nap may get a bit later and last for about an hour and a half and, very soon afterward, he will drop his afternoon nap. Toward the age of three, the nap will shrink again to about an hour, with between 11 and 12 hours of sleep at night.

Daytime cues

Giving the right cues about daytime and nighttime can help a baby along the road to seeing nighttime as the main time for sleeping.

During the day it helps to keep living rooms brightly lit. Give the baby lots of playing and interaction—this is something Grandma can help with. Talk to your grandchild and make eye contact, go for outings, make as much household noise as is necessary, make big rituals of mealtimes and feeding times. During naptimes, keep household noise at a natural level.

Nighttime cues

A baby needs to learn that nighttime is dark, quiet, and tranquil so he should be put down in a darkened room after a calming wind-down bedtime ritual. Your daughter will keep his nighttime feedings as quiet and brief as possible and only change his diaper when really necessary.

If you go to your grandchild at night, don't talk, don't pick him up unless you have to, and keep the lights switched off. Stay as short a time as possible and be businesslike. He'll soon learn that this is not a time for play.

Plenty of sleep
Young babies need lots of sleep and, unless he is hungry, cold, or uncomfortable, a baby will probably be asleep 60 percent of the time.

Sleep safety

One of the many things you'll find has changed since your day is the guidelines on sleep safety. Since the early 1990s, when a great deal of research suggested ways of preventing SIDS (Sudden Infant Death Syndrome), instances have plummeted, even though no specific causes have been found. We now know a great deal about risk factors, and your family can take steps to lower the risk simply by following the latest advice.

Latest guidelines

We know far more about SIDS now than when our children were young and some of the advice may be unfamiliar to you. The precautions that I'm going to outline came out of research into the causes and prevention of SIDS, which still affects one in 2,000 babies. Your children will know about these, but it's important for you to be well informed too.

Always lay a baby down on her back to sleep

Do this from the beginning for both day and night sleeping. This is because babies lose a lot of heat from their tummy, neck, face, and head—they need to do so to regulate their body temperature. Babies can't bring down their temperature in the same efficient way as adults. Also, by lying on her back a baby's breathing isn't impeded. If, at the age of five or six months, the baby persistently turns onto her front, don't become obsessive about turning her over.

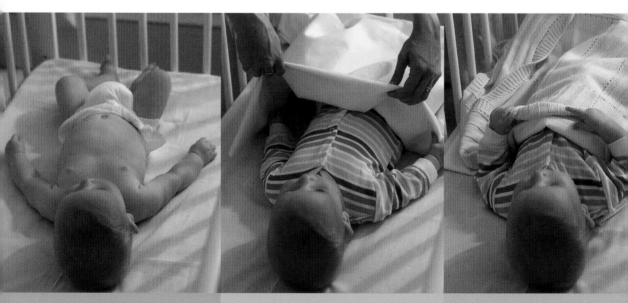

Place the baby feet to foot　　**Arrange bedding at the foot too**　　**Don't use too many cove**

Feet to foot

A baby should be placed with her feet to the foot of the crib. This way, even if she wiggles up the crib, she won't reach the top and cut down the amount of heat that is lost from her head. And make sure that the bedding is arranged so that it's at the foot of the crib as well.

A cool room

It's better to keep the room cool than hot for the reasons I've mentioned—a baby can't regulate her body temperature efficiently. So, except when it's very cold, a baby's bedroom should be a little cooler than the rest of the house, at around 64° F (18° C). Don't bury your grandchild under blankets. A sheet and a couple of blankets is usually enough if the room is kept between 61–64° F (16–18° C).

> **"** *If a baby has a fever or is unwell, get in touch with the doctor immediately, particularly if you notice breathing difficulties* **"**

Smoking and babies

We all now know that smoking around a young baby increases the risk of SIDS, and the greater the exposure, the greater the risk. So the house rule is that smokers can't smoke in the house, and absolutely not in the baby's room. I used to go as far as saying that smokers couldn't hold my babies because the tars and nicotine from cigarettes become impregnated in a smoker's clothes, skin, and hair and I didn't want my baby inhaling these toxic chemicals.

Things to watch for

If a baby has a fever or is unwell, get in touch with the doctor immediately, particularly if you notice any breathing difficulties or the baby is more sleepy than usual.

Sharing a bed

Very young babies who share a bed with their parents have a higher risk of SIDS. This applies mainly to babies whose parents smoke, who have been drinking, are on medication, or are excessively tired. Research tells us that it's best not to bring a new baby into the parents' bed for the first eight weeks because this is when she's at the highest risk of SIDS.

Latest approaches to sleep problems

Experts know much more about sleep now than in our day. So understanding something about the whys and wherefores will help you see the rationale behind some modern practices that your own children may want to adopt.

Old and new approaches

Not all the fashionable approaches to sleep problems will strike you as new. Some, such as swaddling, you may have used yourself. But others are 21st century and your children may adopt any of them or devise a particular style that is all their own and combines elements of several. Parents these days tend to be more precise in analyzing problems than we were, and they come up with more formal and structured solutions.

"Parents today tend to be more precise in analyzing sleep problems than we were, and they come up with more formal and structured solutions"

A sleep journal

One useful tool is a sleep journal, which helps indentify the difficulty and, by doing so, opens up possible ways of dealing with it. There are other payoffs to a sleep journal, like removing personal blame for sleep problems—once you track precisely what's going on, everyone can stop getting worked up and be more objective. You can spot a trend early and take avoiding action. It's easy to assess whether your grandchild is getting enough sleep by totting up the figures, but a journal will also show where and when he sleeps. Best of all, it makes you see what the family may be doing to help or hinder the baby's sleeping patterns.

Most sleep journals have the same form and can be recorded on a sheet of paper or in a book. Everyone in the house who takes care of your grandchild should be familiar with it and contribute. These timings can be filled in for a week, by which time everyone should see a pattern emerging.

Sleep diary entries:
- Time the baby wakes
- Time and length of naps during the day
- Time you start preparing the baby for bed at night
- Time he goes to bed in the evening
- Time he went to sleep
- Time(s) he woke in the night
- What you did
- Time he went back to sleep.

What might emerge from a sleep diary

The following points are the sort of things that a children's sleep clinic in the UK, (*Teach Your Child to Sleep*), observed, and you could help look out for them in your grandchild. Simply analyzing these kinds of findings can point the way to remedial action and how to teach your grandchild comfortable sleep habits.

- Too early rising, leading to many naps during the day
- First nap too early and too long
- Midday nap too early and too short, so he needs an extra nap too close to bedtime
- Three naps could be too many, depending on the baby's age
- Difficult to get the baby back to sleep during the first sleep hours
- Starting bedtime routine too early
- Rewarding baby for waking—for instance, giving him a hug or feeding him
- Nighttime feedings—none are necessary at nine months and later.

Smile at your grandchild
However frazzled and tired you might be, always try to present a smiling face to your grandchild when you go to him. If you smile at him, he will smile back and everything will feel worthwhile.

Lay the baby on the folded blanket

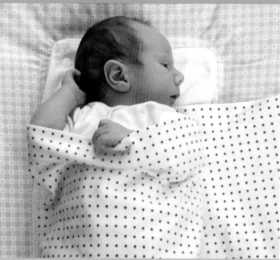

Fold one side over him and tuck it under

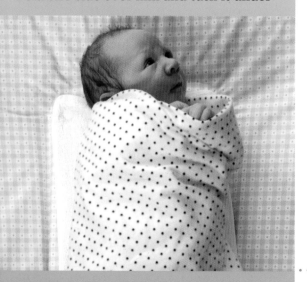

Fold over the other side and tuck it in

Swaddling

You'll remember from your own days as a mom that swaddling or wrapping a young baby in a wrap or blanket can help him sleep; the sensation of being tightly enclosed gives babies a great feeling of security. It's also a useful way of calming a distressed baby. To swaddle a baby, you need a wrap or small light blanket.

- Fold the blanket in half to form a triangle and lay the baby on it, aligning his head with the center of the longest edge.
- Fold one point of the blanket across the baby and tuck it firmly behind his back. Do the same with the other point.
- Tuck the bottom of the blanket back under the baby's feet to keep them covered. Always make sure his head is uncovered and his arms are free, then put him in his bed on his back.

The close wrapping holds the baby's arms in a comfortable position that feels safe and secure, and may also help him sleep longer. If his limbs move while he's asleep, he is less likely to wake if swaddled.

Some babies don't like being swaddled, so don't worry if your grandchild doesn't. Keep a close eye on him when he's swaddled and check his temperature by touching his skin. Unwrap him right away if he feels or looks too hot. Never cover his head when swaddling and only use thin materials.

As you know, swaddling is only appropriate for babies up to about 10 weeks. After that, a baby will quickly get his arms free and kick off the swaddling clothes with his legs.

Sleep techniques

There are a number of techniques for encouraging babies to sleep that your children might want to try. You might not agree with all of them—one that I certainly don't agree with is controlled crying (see pages 101–2)—but as a grandparent your role is to go along with what your children want and support them. The more you understand about what is going on, the better.

Shush and pat

This is something that might strike you as natural and as something any grandma would do instinctively—and it is. It's just that it's been formalized into a soothing sleep aid.

Any woman who's ever had to comfort an upset baby will automatically hold the baby upright with the baby's head on her shoulder, gently rock the baby up and down, pat her back and say shush, shush.

This simple technique will quiet most babies under 10 weeks. They stop crying while listening to the loudish shush and feeling the firm rhythmic pats—they forget to cry. Shushing and patting can also be used to teach a baby of a few weeks old to quiet herself in her crib, which could be a solution to many problems, including getting a baby on to a real sleeping schedule.

The idea is to try to quiet the baby by swaddling, and then spend a few minutes simply sitting quietly with her on your knee. If she cries, shush and pat with her upright on your shoulder. When she stops crying, keep on shushing and patting for a few more pats, then put her in her crib and hold her on her side so you can continue patting her back.

"Shushing and patting a young baby is something any grandma does instinctively. It's just that it's now been formalized into a soothing sleep aid"

Don't stop shushing and patting just because she's silent. Keep on so that she can sink into a deeper and deeper sleep. Shush and pat for at least five minutes. Let the pats get softer and the shushing quieter and then gradually stop and lay her on her back. Don't leave the room. This is to cover the eventuality that she may jerk awake as she's dropping off, and re-starting the shush and pat will ease her back into her sleep without her getting upset.

Young babies have very good memories and can remember feelings. They can remember the feeling of dropping-off to sleep, secure and tranquil, and gradually learn to re-create that feeling and go to sleep unaided. This will happen only if you teach her how to do it, not by letting her cry it out. If she cries seriously again, put her back on your shoulder and shush and pat.

"*After quieting your grandchild, put her in her crib. If she cries, pat her gently, but don't say anything, then leave the room*"

Rapid return

This is somewhere between shush and pat (see page 125) and controlled crying (see pages 101–2). It's less hands-on than shush and pat but more humane than controlled crying and good for babies of four months and older.

After quieting your grandchild with holding, shushing, and patting, and sitting calmly with her on your knee, you put her in her crib. If she cries, you pat her gently but don't say anything, then leave the room. If she cries again, you wait 30 seconds and go silently into the room; don't put on the light, don't speak, just pat her to let her know you're there, then leave again.

You repeat this until your grandchild goes to sleep, possibly lengthening the interval by a few seconds, but only up to a minute or so. You may have to return many times on the first night, fewer on the second and third, and soon your grandchild will have learned to fall asleep on her own.

> **"** *Gradual retreat involves the parent or grandparent gradually distancing themselves from the child a little at a time* **"**

Gradual retreat

This kind of technique is good for an anxious child and involves the parent or caregiver gradually distancing themselves from the child a little at a time as she goes to sleep, to give the child a chance to adjust to separation. Each move should be repeated for three or four nights and at nap times.

It might go like this:
- Sit by your grandchild's crib or bed
- Sit on a chair across the room
- Sit by the door
- Sit outside the door
- Sit out of sight.

There's hardly any crying with this approach, though it may take a month to be fully effective. You might want to reinforce each move with a chart to act as both source of pride and to spur you on. Don't leave your grandchild's room before she's been asleep for a good 10 minutes, otherwise if she wakes and you're not there you'll have broken her trust and will have to start again.

Sleep rituals

I'm a serious believer in sleep rituals, mainly because, if they become a good habit early, they ensure that a baby feels secure and goes to sleep happily. With my own children, my goal was always to have happy bedtimes. This meant, occasionally, that I would overlook misdemeanors because I wanted the hour or so before my children were going down to sleep to be free of tears and upset. I feel the same with my grandchildren.

Battles at bedtime

Sometimes a baby doesn't go to sleep in his crib from birth and will only settle if breast-fed to sleep or held in the arms of his mother or father. Battles may also be caused by leaving a baby to cry for long periods so he becomes extremely unsettled and unhappy in his crib. This teaches a baby to fight sleep. Very often, where there's a bedtime battle, a baby is chronically sleep deprived and will only fall asleep out of sheer exhaustion. There are secondary effects to this—for example, days often start late and naptimes become chaotic. A child who engages in bedtime battles is really begging for a good bedtime routine and a regular time for bed.

The bedtime routine

In some of my grandchildren's families the bedtime ritual really starts with dinner at about 5.30pm. Toward 6pm the children know that Mommy or Daddy or Grandma will go upstairs to run the bath. When dinner is over, everyone scampers upstairs to the bathroom where there can be fun and games undressing, throwing toys into the bath, and generally horsing around.

"A child who engages in bedtime battles is really begging for a good bedtime routine and a regular time for bed. He can become sleep deprived"

While bath time can be rather noisy and carefree, the children do know that they are set on a timetable that will end up with them going to bed in their cribs within half an hour. During bath time there are all sorts of other tiny rituals—playing with the fish under water; pouring water from pitcher to mug; sticking alphabet letters on the sides of the bath; possibly hairwashing. Bath time always ends with tooth brushing.

Even brushing teeth can have its own ritual. Like mine, your grandchild might like to sit on Mommy or Grandma's knee while his teeth are brushed for him. Or he might want to try standing on a little stool so he can see himself in the mirror while having making an effort at brushing his own teeth.

With my grandchildren, climbing out of the bath can be another ritual. Then we choose the towel to dry each child; select a terry-cloth robe to put on before running along the corridor to the bedroom; and choose which brush to use to brush hair. Once in the bedroom there are more rituals: creaming the skin, a little bit of baby massage perhaps, putting on the diaper, and choosing pajamas to put on.

Winding down for the night

Most important of all, we then have the grand ritual of picking out two or three books to read and deciding where to read them. Some nights the grandchildren take turns sitting on my lap; or we might all cuddle up on the sofa together. I always painstakingly point out all the interesting names and pictures right to the end of the book.

It's a good idea to warn a small child that this is "the last book," "the last page," and it's nice to help this wind-down part of the bedtime ritual with some gentle music. But once books are read, it's bedtime.

The next phase is to darken the room and turn down the covers of the crib or bed. The actual going to bed can have a ritual all of its own with special songs—your grandchild choosing which songs he'd like you to sing. Then I give a quick kiss goodnight and a hug, and say, "Sweet dreams. See you in the morning. Good night." I make a smooth exit and close the door.

As they get older, babies like the reassurance of hearing you move around the house. With my own children, I used to keep saying "Good night" as I left the room and went down the stairs so my voice got fainter and fainter, and I do the same when I'm taking care of my grandchildren.

Fun and games at bath time

Brushing teeth

Bedtime story

Bedtimes

A child's sleep needs vary during the first six years of her life, but not as much as many new parents think. As you will probably remember, at 12 months a baby is only sleeping two-and-a-half hours during the day and 11½ during the night. Thereafter, daytime sleeps become shorter, with a two-year-old taking a nap for an hour or so but sleeping nearly 12 hours at night.

Sleep needs

At three, your grandchild may sleep for an hour in the day or drop the nap entirely and sleep about 11 hours during the night. In years four, five, and six, sleep is between 11 and 12 hours, then 11 hours, and then at six years old, just under 11.

Bedtimes are really established so that a child gets the requisite amount of sleep during the night and can be happy, active, eat well, play, and run around during the day. At three years old, in order to get 11 hours of sleep, a child shouldn't be going to bed much after 7 pm and, after very active days, will probably sleep a full 12 hours. By the time a child is four or five, the bedtime might be advanced to 7.30pm but no later. Many children get extremely tired toward 6.30 pm, and at 7 pm are ready for that bedtime ritual.

"Bedtimes are really established to give a child the requisite amount of sleep at night so that they can be happy, active, and eat and play well during the day"

Atmosphere

The atmosphere and the environment in which a baby goes to sleep should be conducive to sleep. Many parents feel that a darkened room, if not a completely pitch black one, is the most appropriate setting for a child to settle down to sleep. What I consider to be very important is that this atmosphere, whatever it is, is consistent, whether there's the addition of a nightlight for comfort or some music to encourage the child to settle down. That means that a child should enjoy the same environment away from home when she comes to stay with you. That may involve, as it has with me, having blackout blinds installed on my bedroom windows, and special curtains.

It's useful to have the room darkened because if children wake early, they can be told it's still nighttime and sleep must continue. They're amenable to being settled down again. Early risers can also be handled by having the same conditions as they have at home, such as an alarm clock or light that signifies it's getting-up time. If you have your grandchild to stay with you or take your grandchild away on vacation, these are some of the accessories you're going to need to make both bedtimes and mornings pleasant.

I don't believe that all household noises should cease when a child goes
to bed. In fact, a young baby may find the sound of household noises like
the dishwasher, the washing machine, or even the vacuum quite reassuring.
But I think it's important that the noise levels are kept reasonably muted after
the child's gone to bed.

Entertaining herself

Once a child has made the transition from crib to bed and is able to get
out of her bed, it's a good idea to encourage her to play in her bedroom by
having lots of her favorite toys in her bedroom and some books to look at.

Playing by herself
Children need to learn
to entertain themselves.
You can help by giving
your grandchild ideas
for imaginative play and
games, then standing
back and letting her
get on with it.

Knowing the signs

Do you remember with your own children how you learned to spot the signs of overtiredness, after which it was much harder to get them to sleep? Everyone who takes care of a baby needs to be on the lookout for his particular signs of being tired. These signs are slightly different in all babies and caregivers need to watch the baby closely to make sure that they know what to look out for.

Sleep window

The sleep window extends from the time that a baby shows the first signs of being tired to the time he goes to sleep easily. If he goes beyond the signs of being tired he becomes overtired and irritable. During the sleep window, it's possible to put a baby down and for him to fall into a deep sleep in a short time. If the sleep window is missed, a baby may become fretful and upset as he gets more and more tired, so it's much more difficult for him to go down peacefully.

" There's a journey that begins with a baby's first yawn and ends with him finally dropping off into a deep sleep "

Watching and acting

I like Tracy Hogg's approach to sleep, which she describes in her wonderful book *The Baby Whisperer*. She sees going to sleep not as an event but more like a journey that begins with the baby's first yawn and ends with him finally dropping off into a deep sleep. What we have to realize is that we adults have to help him to get there. And we do that by recognizing his sleep window and helping him to wind down. With your experience of parenting, you'll probably find this easier than your children do and it's something you can help with by pointing out the signs.

If you watch your grandchild closely, you'll get to know what he looks like when he's tired and then you have to act on it immediately. So study what the baby does when he's tired. In a very young baby, a yawn is often the strongest clue, but your grandchild might also fuss and make jerky movements with his head, arms, and legs. He may begin to squeak and, by the time he's got control of his head at around six or seven weeks, he may turn his head away from you or from the toy that you're playing with.

If you're carrying him he'll burrow his face into your neck. He's telling you that he needs to sleep and your responsibility is to act promptly and help him do that. It's worth acting quickly because it makes it easy for him to learn the skills of settling down. Once you spot the signs, the window of opportunity is already closing. And if you miss the sleep window or try to stretch it out, mistakenly thinking that he'll sleep longer at night, it will take longer to get him to sleep because he will be overtired. An older baby can keep himself awake, even when he's actually quite sleepy. He then becomes so tired and tense that sleep is impossible.

Look for a pattern

If you find it difficult to recognize when your grandchild is getting tired, keeping a sleep journal (see pages 122–3) may help you and your children to pick up his messages. Simply jot down what's going on at the time the baby goes to sleep and how he behaves before going down. After three or four days you'll begin to see a pattern emerging and you'll be able to spot your grandchild's own little sleep messages and make bedtimes easier.

Another thing you can do is help your grandchild love his crib. A baby spends a long time there and it will make his life a misery if he resists being put down. So it's up to us to help him. After recognizing that your grandchild is tired, one of the kindest things you can do is to help him wind down for a few moments before settling him into his crib. Loving his "wind down" routine is the first step to loving his crib.

Dealing with sleep problems

I get hundreds of letters from parents—and grandparents—desperate for advice on how to improve children's sleep habits. Based on my own experience, I've always believed that setting a good sleep routine is too important to wait until children have reached school age. Ideally, the routine should begin in the first weeks of life—and that means starting to build good habits.

So I'm not surprised that new research has found that children who are consistently allowed to stay up past their bedtime have a higher risk of late-night sleeplessness for the rest of their lives. It seems that late nights watching television or playing computer games affect children's body clocks more profoundly than adults', and the effects are hard to reverse. Here are some common problems I've encountered, both from readers and in my own family.

Children wake Mom and Dad up too early

Sleep solution: Help teach children about private time From as early an age as possible, help your grandchildren to learn about privacy. You can do this by taking them to the bathroom and standing outside, explaining it's to give them privacy. Do this and they'll soon accept that their parents' bedroom is sometimes a no-go zone. For example, at weekends, you can say it's only OK to go in to Mom and Dad after a certain time. You can buy wonderful toy clocks that use symbols such as a sun, or a rabbit opening its eyes, to signal "getting-up" time, to help teach them this. I've tried this with my own granddaughters, who will happily lie there watching the rabbit until it's time to get up.

"Try to resettle children without actually taking them out of bed, and certainly not out of the bedroom. This does require patience "

Not sleeping through the night

Sleep solution: Help children feel secure Don't resort to picking them up and cuddling them for long periods, or playing, since they will just learn to associate these daytime activities with nighttime—when what you want to instill is that night is for sleeping. If a child is very upset stay with her, stroke her while she's in the crib or bed, and talk soothingly until she drops off. Babies and toddlers need to feel secure and that Mom, Dad, or Grandma is there if necessary.

Try to resettle children without actually taking them out of bed, and certainly not out of the bedroom. This technique does require patience and may mean you're going back and forth a lot to start with, but it really works—perhaps this is something Grandma can help with while Mom and Dad get some sleep?

"Buy your grandchild his own special clock so he can see when it is getting-up time"

Wanting to sleep with you

Sleep solution: Be firm Snuggling up with parents or grandparents is the best thing ever as far as young children are concerned, but let them sleep with you a few times and they'll never want to sleep in their own bed, so be strict. You might love it, but Mom and Dad won't thank you. If your grandchild does wander into your bedroom, get up and put her back into her own bed. Explain that grown-ups need their privacy at night.

Waking with night terrors

Sleep solution: Don't worry During a night terror, children appear awake and may call out or thrash around, but they're actually in a trancelike state and don't know you're there. Although it can be worrying to watch, these terrors are a phase that many children go through and soon grow out of. Don't try to wake her up or hold her, since she'll probably push you away. Simply stand back watch for 10 minutes or so, making sure she's OK, before leaving her to sleep.

Sweet dreams
A bedtime ritual could start with a drink of milk, taking a bath, getting into pajamas, being read to, going into the bedroom, singing a song, then a kiss goodnight.

Toddler tantrums at bedtime

Sleep solution: Develop a bedtime ritual This can start 30–45 minutes before bed and should be the same every night. If Mom and Dad are short of time, this is an ideal time for Grandma to help.

"Should I get paid for childcare?"

Sally is 54 and gave up work early so she could help her son and daughter-in-law care for their first child. They're saving for a down payment on their first house and both work. Sally wanted to help them get on the property ladder and loves taking care of her grandson. She's aware that money is tight for her son's family but it is for her now too, since her husband has been laid off. She's regretting the loss of the money from her job and wants to ask her son to pay her something for her time.

as providers of free child care and many grandparents do give their services free out of love for their grandchildren.

It's hard to go back on an arrangement that's existed for some time, but I think payment should be part of any form of regular child care that involves more than the occasional day—unless you're comfortable enough not to need the money.

What's more, Sally gave up her job to devote herself to her grandson, so I think she has every right to payment of some kind. Perhaps Sally's son doesn't realize how tight

I think payment should be part of any form of regular child care unless you don't need the money. Sally should talk to her son and settle this once and for all

Some would say that Sally's son and daughter-in-law are taking advantage of her generous nature and of course she should be paid. Sally gave up her job to help them and they should have offered to make some of that money up to her. Since they haven't, perhaps Sally should just ask?

Keep in mind, though, that money's always a difficult topic, especially when involving family, and in situations such as grandparents doing child care for their children. Parents often see grandparents

money is since his father's lay-off. It might be time for Sally to explain this to her son and his family.

Any payment has to be mutually agreed upon, since Sally doesn't want to make life difficult for her children by asking for too much. She could ask another grandma what she gets paid or look for information on grandparenting websites. Then I would suggest Sally comes clean and has a family powwow with her husband, son, and daughter-in-law to settle it once and for all.

7 *Learning and Play*

Play is all-important for a young child, and with your patience and devotion you can be your grandchild's ideal playmate and teacher.

Playing and learning with Grandma

You are your grandchild's ideal playmate. You spent years playing with your own children so you know instinctively how to entertain, amuse, and join in game playing. To a new baby and to a toddler, preschool child, and all the way up to a teenager, *play is learning*. Playing isn't a trivial pursuit; it's very hard work.

Growing and learning

During play, a baby grows and develops in every way and all directions. Fortunately, babies come equipped with an overwhelming desire to play, which helps us help them to grow, develop, and learn.

Your special kind of play is important because it not only encourages adventurousness and independence but also helps your grandchild, from birth, to explore his senses—sight, sound, taste, touch, smell—as well as movement and speech. Every time a small baby uses any of his senses he *thinks*. And every time he thinks he grows half a million brain connections per second!

So when you tickle his fingers or toes with a fluffy toy, he grows at least half a million brain connections. The same thing happens when you chatter together at close quarters and he sees you smiling and bobbing your head, when you wiggle his arms and legs while he's lying on a changing mat, or when you play with water in his bath. You're his teacher par excellence. It's impossible to overestimate the importance of play to babies and young children. It's the basis of all learning. And if you're an active grandparent you can help lay the

Interaction
Babies respond so well to the loving interest of their grandparents and everyone gains from any kind of interaction —from fun while changing a diaper to games at bath time.

You are an expert

As a grandparent, because of your experience, the life you've led, and your range of interests and hobbies, you can stimulate your grandchild in a way that a parent can't. Your grandchild will learn very easily from you, and I'm sure that, like me, you will get huge satisfaction from the hours you spend playing and learning together.

- You have a caring interest in him, which he can sense because it makes him feel special—the perfect setting for new games and new skills.
- You have the time to play until your grandchild gets bored.
- You take obvious delight in his tiniest achievement and make him feel confident.
- Nothing is too much trouble for you so games can extend his concentration and foster his curiosity.
- You are endlessly patient and show him how to try, try, try again until he succeeds, then *praise* him.

A wonderful way to bond
Playing with your grandchildren and helping them learn and develop skills can be so much fun, and a wonderful way to bond with them.

foundations for your grandchild's secure and happy development. All you have to do to help a skill develop is to take your lead from your grandchild. This is the golden and unbreakable rule.

And your grandchild will always show you with some sign that he wants to, and can, move on. It's important to follow his lead because, if you do, you'll hit exactly the right moment when it's essential for him to acquire the skill.

Teachable moments

Ever since I read about "teachable moments" I've believed they're the easiest and most enjoyable way to teach a child anything. And you, as a grandparent, will have more teachable moments with your grandchild, than even her parents, because you have the time and the desire to pass on snippets of information wherever you are.

Take every opportunity

A teachable moment arises out of an ordinary everyday activity or situation where you feel that there's an opportunity to explain something. This might be an idea, how something works, why something is important, how we do things, an answer to a question, pointing out something interesting, a new word, a new sensation, a new feeling.

"A teachable moment arises out of an ordinary everyday activity or situation where you feel that there's an opportunity to explain something"

Unsurprisingly children love these moments. The setting is informal, it doesn't feel like teaching, and best of all it's piecemeal, which is how children learn anyway. It's appealing to a child because a teachable moment has its own logic. Here are some teachable moments that I've experienced with my grandchildren recently.

- You're "gardening" together and you see a worm. You can talk about how worms aerate the soil and turn it over (as worm casts), and how a worm has no eyes because it's always in the dark.

- You're crossing a street with traffic lights. Here's a good opportunity to talk about the light sequence and how RED means STOP and GREEN means GO. Extend this to talking about how you should look left, then right, then left again, then cross.

- It's bath time, and as your grandchild gets into the bath the water rises, then when she stands up, the level drops. You explain why and you could mention Archimedes and "Eureka." You explain how some things float and some things sink.

- You use a word that might be difficult for a toddler or young child to understand—for instance, words such as recognize, reflection (in the mirror), camouflage—and then immediately explain what it means and give examples of how to use it.

- Use every opportunity to explain a concept—this is hard, but this is soft; a cat meows but a dog barks; birds fly and so do airplanes.

A shared interest
Encourage a child's interest in growing things and the environment. You never know—you might even create an eco-warrior by sharing a hobby such as gardening.

Your grandchild's personality

No doubt you remember how you used to say that your own children were as different as day and night. Through your own children you learned how to nurture different personality traits, so now you're fully equipped to help your grandchild develop his own individuality. Your grandchild's personality is much more dependent on what he learns from his family than anything inherited.

Helping your grandchild's development

Many features of your grandchild's personality will affect his future prospects, such as the ability to relate to people and get along; the ability to learn from mistakes; the willingness to jump in and work hard; the powers to observe, concentrate, inquire; the ability to be creative, thorough, determined, and ambitious. All these will help a child and you're ideally placed to reinforce those traits. You can also do much to strengthen inborn traits such as independence, responsiveness (a "ready" smile), thoroughness, a gentle nature, self-reliance.

" We now know that boys and girls develop differently. At birth, a girl's brain is ahead of a boy's, and she develops slightly faster "

A "difficult" grandchild is often responding normally to a difficult family set up. You have a special role to play here. A calm grandparent who takes everything in her stride can mollify a difficult child and transform him.

Should you treat boys and girls differently?

Research has shown that boys and girls develop differently. At birth, a girl's brain is ahead of a boy's, and subsequently she develops slightly faster. If you're aware of these differences, you can concentrate on your grandchild's strengths and encourage her or him positively in less able areas.

I'm pointing out the differences not to suggest one gender is superior to the other, but to give you special insight into how your grandchild ticks. Understanding boy/girl differences will help you to choose games that foster those aspects of your grandchild's development that need special attention. As a busy parent, you probably didn't have time to do this, but as a grandparent with more time you'll notice that girls are born with two advantages over boys.

Talking The verbal centers in the left side of a girl's brain are further along the skill map than those in a boy's, so anything to do with language is generally acquired earlier in girls. As a loving grandma to a boy, you can encourage him with lots of songs and clapping games.

Emotional understanding The two sides of a girl's brain have already developed connections at birth (these connections aren't in place in boys until nine months), allowing girl babies to be more comfortable with their emotions and sensitive to the feelings of those around them. Your job as an attentive grandma is to help your grandson deal with his emotions and not to get angry and frustrated.

Your special brand of help

When you're with your grandchild, you'll know that it's a good idea to be over the top, dramatic, and theatrical as you talk and play. Laugh, giggle, and hug as much as you like, and keep eye contact with him whenever you can, especially when he's very young.

With talking

- Be very verbal—and speak clearly
- Sing lots of songs
- Play lots of clapping and action games
- Play classical music.

With emotions

- Give plenty of physical contact
- Emphasize success with praise
- Deal promptly with anger, fear, and frustration
- Treat boys and girls in exactly the same way when they cry or need consoling —it's never right to expect a little boy to suppress his feelings "because he's a boy."

Talk all the time
Keep talking, talking, talking as you play—it helps your grandchild learn to speak, which is the most complex of all human skills and the key to communication and language.

How your grandchild develops

Your grandchild's best playmates are his parents and his grandparents. It's you he responds to most readily and it's with you that he lays the foundations for his secure and happy development. If you know how your grandchild is going to grow in his first year, you'll easily be able to devise games that promote his development. And you'll instinctively know which toys help him reach his full potential.

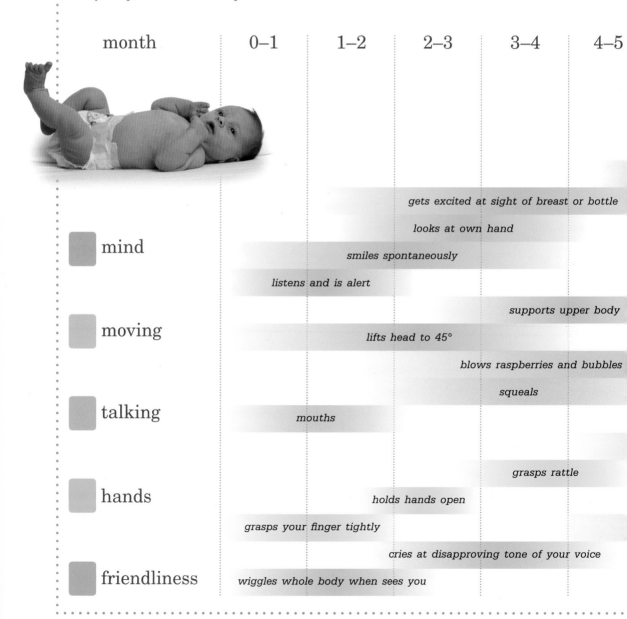

month	0–1	1–2	2–3	3–4	4–5
mind			gets excited at sight of breast or bottle		
			looks at own hand		
		smiles spontaneously			
	listens and is alert				
moving				supports upper body	
		lifts head to 45°			
talking				blows raspberries and bubbles	
				squeals	
		mouths			
hands				grasps rattle	
		holds hands open			
	grasps your finger tightly				
friendliness			cries at disapproving tone of your voice		
	wiggles whole body when sees you				

Month-by-month with your grandchild

Your grandchild's main skills are laid out below to give you some idea of when you can expect each skill to emerge, though the timetable is very flexible. When your grandchild has acquired a skill, he's reached one of his "milestones."

Remember that until one skill is learned he can't go on to the next, so you'll help him if you play games that encourage the emergence of skills just at the right time.

5–6	6–7	7–8	8–9	9–10	10–11	11–12

shows you things in a book and shakes head for "no"

waves goodbye

holds arms out

understands "no"

stands and cruises

crawls

sits unsupported

says "dada" and "mama" with meaning

says syllables "da" and "ma"

stacks blocks

bangs blocks together

points—then grasps with thumb and finger

grabs with one hand

reaches out

loves theatrical show of emotions, laughs at "jokes"

plays clapping games

touches your face and touches another baby

Games to play

Armed with a rough road map of how your grandchild is going to grow and develop in the first year, it's easy for you to think up games that can help her dormant skills to emerge and flower.

First steps

If you want to help your two-week-old granddaughter learn to walk, encourage her to lift her head while lying on her tummy. Head control is the first step on the road to walking, even though the two events are separated by a year or more. You can help by playing games in which she has to try to lift her head.

Similarly, when your six-month-old grandchild blows raspberries at you, answer her in the same way because blowing raspberries is early training for speech. And at 10 months, when your grandchild tries to pick up peas between finger and thumb, encourage her because that pincer grip is a prewriting skill.

If you want to, you can be one of your grandchild's "blueprints" for life. In their early years, children view adults, particularly those they see frequently, as role models and imitate them in everything. If you smile a lot and you are gentle, kind, patient, and forgiving, your grandchild can learn all of those qualities simply by imitating you.

Play, newborn to six months

Talking is one of the best forms of play for infants so start talking to your grandchild and never stop. Describe everything you do, use a singsong voice, and use the inclusive "we"—as in, we play like this, we do that. Here are some other ways of encouraging the development of your grandchild at this stage:

Toys

- Mobiles for sight and hand–eye coordination
- Baby gym for sight and hand–eye coordination
- Squeezing and squashing toys to grasp and put in her mouth
- Soft toys for different textures
- Rattles, bells, and squeakers that teach cause and effect.

Early talking

Sing lullabies while cuddling, or rocking your grandchild to sleep.

Let's get physical

Dance, rock, and sway back and forth to the beat of simple, melodic tunes. Simple games babies enjoy include baby sit-ups, knee rides, and galloping around the room (gently and always with the baby well supported).

Play, 7–12 months

It's a good idea to concentrate on handling skills at this stage. Here are some ideas for games that help your grandchild learn to grasp, push, pull, and make pincer hand movements.

Toys

- Freestanding rattle to bat for hand–eye coordination
- Tops
- Balls to hold and throw
- Toy trucks, cars, and animals that move
- Cloth books
- Cloth blocks
- Floating toys and books for the bath.

Encourage speech

Blow into empty paper rolls, imitate animal sounds, and sing songs such as "Old MacDonald Had a Farm" and "Patty-Cake."

Be active

More active games, such as piggyback rides and leg lifts, are enjoyable for most older babies. Ball-rolling can be started. Hiding games, such a "Peek-A-Boo" and "Which Hand?" (hide an object in your hand so it can be easily found, and let her choose the correct one; praise her when she guesses right) will appeal to her sense of curiosity.

Playing indoors/outdoors

Banging a pot and lid, hitting wooden spoons (these can be taped to reduce noise) against the bottom of a pot; sifting small amounts of flour; and filling empty canisters, cans, and boxes with wooden clothespins or blocks, are all fun and provide lessons in sound making.

Help her play with a ball

Provide toys that encourage hand skills

Banging pans teaches cause and effect

Play, 12–18 months

Creative play is very good for children in this age group. You can experiment with all sorts of materials together—never mind the mess. Encourage her to feel proud of what she does by putting her pictures up on the fridge.

Toys

- Tambourine
- Musical box
- Very simple puzzles
- Colored chalks and crayons
- Baby walker
- Building blocks
- Books with textures and colors
- Pull-and-push toys.

Talking

She'll be starting to say one or two words with meaning and asking for things. Continue singing nursery rhymes, which are excellent for language development. Talk to your grandchild as often as possible, using adult speech, not "baby talk."

Be energetic

Simple movement games like "Ring-Around-the-Rosy," "Follow the Leader," and "Hide and Seek" (make sure you're not too hard to find!) are good to work off some of your grandchild's excess energy.

Start painting

Pasting, coloring, and painting can be done under supervision. Make sure all materials are nontoxic.

Playing inside and outside

Sand boxes and water trays can be hours of fun. Give your grandchild household containers, measuring cups, and bubble-blowing mixtures with wands.

Play, 18–24 months

Children of this age are getting quite smart and like to be stretched. She can now tackle more challenging toys and games with your help, giving her opportunities to show off the new skills she is mastering.

Toys

- Xylophone
- Shape sorters
- Dolls
- Hammering toys
- Telephone
- Pull-along toys
- Playdough
- Musical toys
- Tricycle.

Talking

Read books to your grandchild that have more words, and especially those that rhyme. Make up stories with your grandchild as the heroine. Tell her stories about your childhood.

Physical activities and games

Sing songs with actions: "Itsy Bitsy Spider" and "London Bridge is Falling Down" are entertaining, and can be played with other children. Walk around with your grandchild on a tricycle that you can control with a handle.

Being an artist

Encourage her to make collages using paper, styrofoam, string, rice, fabric, and other materials such as feathers and stones. She'll enjoy finger painting and making scribbles on big pieces of paper as well as simple modeling with playdough. Make sure she does all these things under your supervision.

Play, 2–3½ years

Encourage role playing as an outlet for her emotions—you'll love joining in. And take your grandchild to the library and let her choose books for herself.

Toys

- Paints, crayons
- Safe scissors to master cutting
- Role-playing toys—doctor set, fireman uniform, dolls
- Lego
- Jigsaw puzzles with large pieces (she'll need help with these)
- Dolls, tea sets (for tea parties), cooking sets
- Toy dustpan and brush, vacuum cleaner, or drill, to "help" you.

Speech

Your grandchild is learning new words all the time now. Try alphabet and counting games. Introduce simple tongue twisters and jokes—children love jokes.

Group games

Activities and games that revolve around music, such as "Musical Chairs" or those involving imitation, such as "Simon Says," are now within your grandchild's abilities.

Now is the time to introduce crayon rubbings, spatter painting, and string painting. Your grandchild also can make potato prints and simple stamps from carrots and cut-up sponges.

Indoor/outdoor play

Arrange simple cooking projects and let your grandchild measure out the ingredients. Nature activities, such as discussing rainbows or sowing seeds, should help your grandchild understand her world.

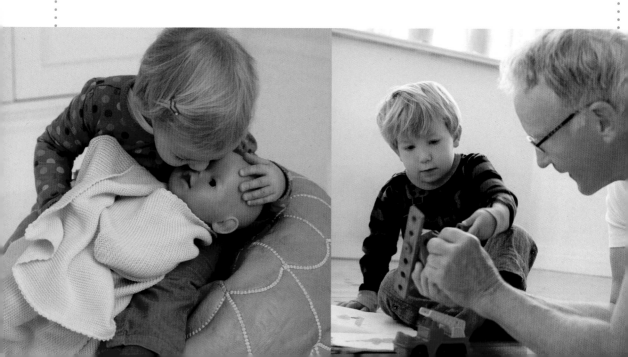

Still playing and learning at 3½–5 years

In addition to playing at home you could also take your grandchild on outings. These will be exciting now that your grandchild is able to appreciate what she sees and remember it.

Toys

- Alphabet toys
- Blackboard and chalk
- Play garages, airports, or stores
- Model vehicles
- Binoculars
- Camera
- Pop-up books
- Table-top mazes
- Bat and ball
- Simple nature study
- Gardening set.

Numbers

You can introduce numbers playfully. Concentrate on number rhymes and counting songs as a form of preschool mathematics play.

Games, games

Board games of a simple variety involving spinning a wheel, throwing dice, or moving pieces will be enjoyed by the child now, as will card games.

Truly artistic

Making simple masks and hand puppets out of paper bags, tights, and fabric is something children of this age can do. Create "furniture," "vehicles," and "play houses" out of cardboard boxes and tubes.

Outings

You can begin to take your grandchild to the movies, theater, and museums featuring shows for children. Visits to zoos and animal parks will also be popular.

Things only you can do

Every grandparent enjoys a unique position in their grandchildren's lives. You don't have to strive to be special. You are special by definition. And you can come into your own as a grandparent if you put your own distinctive stamp on your role by being inimitably who you are. If you do, you'll find you have a devoted fan in your grandchild.

Something to share

Maybe you enjoy an activity (gardening) or a hobby (bird watching) or you have a particular skill (perhaps drawing, knitting, needlework, or playing tennis), which you can share with your grandchildren. This can provide an opportunity for them to accompany you into a world all of your own, one that only you can introduce them to.

The great thing is that you will have boundless enthusiasm for the activity. That's infectious, and your enthusiasm will carry your grandchild with you. You communicate that energy to your grandchildren so that it becomes a thrilling journey you take together, with you as benevolent teacher and your grandchild as willing student.

" *Start doing things with your grandchildren when they're young and they'll grow up thinking of you as an exciting companion* "

Start when they're young

If you enjoy activities together when your grandchild is very young, he'll grow up thinking of you as an exciting companion, someone special who shares special pleasures with him. Children are very sensitive to this act of joyful discovery and, as soon as they're able, they start to bring little gifts of that same kind to you. You form your own virtuous circle, where you respect what each can teach the other, and it will probably last for life. In my own experience I'm constantly surprised and delighted by the way my grandchildren push my interests further than I could have taken them on my own.

And of course you open up your grandchild's world in a way that's special to you. It can be anything, from finding out about insects to stamp collecting or jewelry making—the possibilities are endless.

Do it together

Encourage your grandchild in all sorts of different activities. It's the doing it together that counts.

Planting seeds

A plant pot, used yogurt container, or a small plastic tray is fine for planting seeds together. You can teach your grandchild what plants need to grow—water, sun, and soil, and you can track the seeds' growth at each visit. Choose seeds that grow quickly and dramatically, like purple flowering morning glory. Even better is to collect seeds from seedheads in your garden and plant them. Then your grandchild can get the idea of the circle of life in a very simple and direct way.

Collecting and pressing flowers

I pressed flowers as a teenager as part of my botany studies so I've bought little flower presses for all my grandchildren. We wander around my garden choosing flowers that we want to press, then we fit each one of them into the press. When the flowers have had a chance to dry, we usually make them into a collage of an imaginary garden with glitter and paint that the whole family can admire —a lovely end point.

A small microscope

All my grandchildren enjoy looking at things under a microscope. Dead insects and spiders that we find are a particular favorite. But so are plants. The underside of the leaf of a fern with all the rows of seeds is very exciting when seen in up close. Even newsprint looks thrilling through a microscope.

Plant seeds and watch them grow

Pick flowers for pressing

Teach him how to use a microscope

TV, phones, and computers

Most parents and grandparents worry about children spending too much time in front of the TV (and with good reason). And now there are cell phones and the internet that can displace more worthwhile activities. As grandparents, we might enjoy peace and quiet when our grandkids play computer games or text friends all night—but it's not a good kind of quiet. It's an unnatural stillness that encourages them to retreat into themselves.

Babies need people

Research has shown that there is a direct connection between speech troubles and too much TV. Put a baby in a room with a television on and they're naturally more drawn to the moving images on the screen than real people. But a machine can't teach them to talk. For that they need one-on-one attention from a familiar adult who makes eye contact with them. That's how their brains learn.

"There's a direct connection between speech troubles and too much TV. A baby is drawn to the images on the screen, but a machine can't teach a baby to talk"

Of course cell phones, computers, and video gaming consoles are great new inventions of the digital age—but their overuse by children does worry me. I don't think competitive computer games should ever be in the hands of children under eight, since they're just not emotionally equipped to deal with them.

What you should know when you're supervising your grandchildren

In the past 10 years, there's been a 40 percent rise in the number of children visiting doctors with repetitive strain injury (RSI). It covers a range of conditions that normally only affect adults, in particular those whose job involves repetitive

How much TV?

Of course you can't interfere with the house rules of your children, but when you're in charge these are the guidelines I suggest.

- Up to 3, no TV—watching television at this age has been linked to poor reading and maths skills later.

- 3–5, half an hour a day
- 5–8, an hour a day
- 8–10, one and a half hours a day

movements such as athletes, assembly line workers, or people inputting data into computers. But worryingly we're now seeing RSI in kids as young as five, as a direct result of too much computer gaming and texting.

On top of this, children are having posture problems and back pain—again conditions we used to see only in older people. A study published in Fundamentals of Pediatrics found the incidence of back pain in adolescents is 30%—a figure that might be partly blamed on hours spent in front of the computer in awkward postures.

Explore together
Help your grandchild use computers well by exploring the internet with him. Watch podcasts of swimming sharks, listen to the calls of jungle birds, and travel the world via internet maps.

Why your grandchildren are at risk

Until they reach puberty, children's muscles, tendons, ligaments, and joints are still growing. Too much stress on these areas, as they struggle to adapt to unnatural movements or too much pressure, will affect how they grow. This can lead to sore tendons and muscles, which become enlarged because they have to work harder to deal with the strain. Ligaments can thicken and joints become inflamed, which is the beginning of low-grade arthritis. And if the damage persists, this can progress toward full-blown arthritis.

Battles over television and computer use can cause huge family arguements. So the logical way to avoid conflict, and you can help here, is to ration screen time—before it becomes necessary to impose a ban.

How to ration time without tantrums

This is something you might find tricky when you're taking care of your grandchildren. I suggest the following guidelines, but best of all is to offer the children something better to do. Suggest a visit to the park, read a story, or get out the paints.

- ***Set limits***: It's not fair to let a child become addicted, whether to a computer game or texting on the phone, since once she's settled into a pattern, it's difficult to change her behavior. So with consoles, games, and computers I suggest the same restrictions I do for television. Up to the age of three children shouldn't be allowed near them. Between three and five they should be allowed half an hour a day, rising to an hour a day after five. Set limits early on and a child will understand and be able to cope with the rules.
- ***Family controls***: My advice is to install a parental control on the computer. And no computers or TV in children's bedrooms.
- ***Have screen breaks***: Make sure your grandchildren take a break every 15–20 minutes when they're playing on a games console. This means getting up, stretching, and walking around—not just stopping the game.

"I'm doing too much—how do I tell them?"

Megan is feeling like a glorified nanny. When her first grandchild came along, she was eager to help out and started just babysitting now and then, which she enjoyed. Then Megan's daughter got a part-time job and asked her mom to take the baby for two days a week. While Megan enjoys the contact with her granddaughter, she feels put upon and unappreciated. She didn't expect to be giving up so much time, but how does she tell her daughter and son-in-law that she's doing too much?

days of babysitting. Megan can then explain that she wants to help them and she loves taking care of her granddaughter but that she feels she'd like to do less.

She could ask for their help. Involve them in the solution. What way could they adjust the time she gives them? You never know, given the responsibility for finding a new way of managing Megan's time they could come up with some helpful suggestions.

I know this is difficult because exactly the same thing happened to a friend of mine. And she couldn't bring herself to tell her

Megan needs to tell her daughter and son-in-law
how she feels and involve them in coming up
with a solution that works for everyone

It's easy to see how Megan got into this position. She wanted to help her daughter and son-in-law, as many grandparents like to do, and her role just grew imperceptibly. Now she's nervous to say how she feels in case they take umbrage.

I do think Megan needs to be careful how she approaches the subject, otherwise her daughter and son-in-law may see it as criticism and it could cause tension in the family. Perhaps she could say she'd like to have a chat, perhaps at the end of one of her

daughter how she felt. But her husband did. He was so sick of hearing his wife go on about the time she was spending taking care of their granddaughter and saying that she felt unappreciated that he just came straight out with it to the pair of them.

He didn't find this difficult because he wasn't emotionally involved. And to do them justice the children took it well and have been grateful for any help ever since. My friend feels much happier and even gets the occasional present.

8 Good Times with Grandma & Grandpa

You'll find that outings with your grandchild as well as fun and games at home are as enjoyable for you as for her.

First outings

No baby is too young for an outing with Grandma and Grandpa. In fact, perhaps the easiest time to be out and about with your grandchild is when he's young and portable. A young baby can go just about anywhere and he will enjoy the change of scene, even if he doesn't understand what's going on.

Start with short trips

At first, anything that involves more than a trip to a local store may seem daunting, and even though you're an old hand, you'll probably be a bit nervous and unsure about how your grandchild will react. Try to relax—he'll pick up on any anxieties you have.

Don't be too ambitious—go to your local park, perhaps, or stop off for coffee. Even a short trip like this is fun for you and your grandchild, and gives your daughter some much-needed time to herself. Make sure you're confident about being away from home with your grandchild before you opt for something farther afield. And try to travel at off-peak times when there's less congestion, especially if you're going by bus or train.

Dealing with feeding

If your grandchild is being breast-fed, outings will have to be fit in between feedings, unless you can take some expressed milk with you. If he is bottle-fed, you will find that disposable bottles and prepackaged formulas (see page 54) are a real godsend and make your life much easier.

Once your grandchild is on solids, you'll have to remember to carry food, a feeding dish, a plastic spoon, a bib, a cup with a spout, a supply of liquids, and something for him to nibble on, such as pieces of dry toast or rusks. You can feed him directly from a jar, but remember that whatever he doesn't finish from of a feeding jar must be thrown away afterward, because it's contaminated with saliva, and germs will grow in it very quickly.

What you need to take with you

The better prepared you are for an outing with your grandchild the more successful it will be. This list might look daunting at first, but after the first couple of times you'll have everything on hand and it will become second nature to you.

- Changing bag or mat
- Disposable diapers
- Baby wipes
- Diaper cream
- Plastic bags for dirty diapers
- Disposable bottle and formula if baby is bottle-fed
- Comforter or pacifier if your grandchild uses one
- Feeding equipment and snacks for an older baby
- Sun hat or cold-weather hat
- A sweater
- A few favorite toys and books.

Changing

Even if your grandchild normally wears cloth diapers, forget the expense and take disposable diapers with you on a trip. They're just so convenient, quick, and easy for both you and your grandchild. You can always do the changing on the back seat of the car, or in the trunk if he lies on a rug or a towel. There's generally no need to do any more than sponge bathe while traveling, unless he has an accident. Wipes are essential, as is a bag for dirty diapers.

Using a stroller

We all had strollers or carriages of some kind when our children were young, but the modern versions are very different. Get instructions before you go out alone. You'll need to be adept at collapsing and opening the stroller within a few seconds without any problems, so practice it at home before your first outing. At the very least, you should be able to open it with only one hand, kick it shut with your feet, and know how to operate the brakes—and don't forget you'll have to do all these things while holding the baby. Here are a few safety tips:

Putting on a baby backpack
Using a backpack is a great way of carrying your grandchild if your back is up to it. Make sure you know how to put it on properly—it can be difficult at first without help.

- When you open the stroller always make sure that it's in the fully extended position, with the brakes fully locked.
- Never put your grandchild in the stroller without a safety harness.
- Never ever leave him in a stroller unattended.
- Don't put shopping bags on the handles of the stroller; it can unbalance the stroller and the child may be injured.
- When you stop, always put the brakes on, because you could inadvertently take your hands off the stroller and it could run away.
- Make sure the brakes and catches work well and that the wheels are solid.

Ideas for things to do together

There are lots of activities on offer for grandparents with their grandchildren so there's no need to feel at a loss for ideas.

- Go along to coffee mornings and parent-and-toddler groups.
- Music groups for babies from six months are great fun.
- Water play classes—from 6 months and up. Ask at a local pool about parent-and-baby sessions. They'll welcome grandparents too.
- Baby movement classes may be run at community centers for babies from six months of age and can be an opportunity for bonding.
- Baby massage classes, probably run by a natural health center or local yoga teacher, can bring you very close to your grandchild.
- Find out if there is a baby-gym class in your area. Some centers run these for babies as young as six months and their caregivers.

Shopping with your grandchild

Going out with an active child is much more demanding than with a baby, but it can be lots of fun. Even just a simple shopping trip can be a wonderful opportunity to spend time with your grandchild. Always go well prepared, however. I never leave home with my grandchildren without some drinks and favorite snacks. Take it from me—there's nothing worse than being stuck somewhere with hungry children and the wrong foods!

A chance to learn

You can use shopping trips as opportunities to teach your grandchild all sorts of things—about colors, for example: "This can is red; that package is blue; that jar has a yellow wrapper." Any child will recognize the cereal box which she sees at breakfast every morning and will soon understand what the words mean. From quite an early age, say 18 months, you can say to her, "Do you see the cereal? Now I wonder where the jam is?"

Early reading can be encouraged by teaching your grandchild to associate the contents of a package or can with things that she actually eats at home. For example, if she drinks cocoa regularly, you only have to take the container of the brand she sees everyday from the shelf and ask,"What does this word say?"for her to respond with "cocoa," because she has learned from experience that cocoa is what comes out of that container. All my children began to read food packages before they read anything else.

Shopping safely

Once your grandchild can walk, losing her in a crowd can be a worry, so take some steps to prevent this from happening. Make sure she learns her name, address, and phone number from as early an age as possible just in case she does get lost. You can also:

- Dress her in something colorful, so that you can spot her from a distance.
- Have some sort of family code for your grandchildren to come back to you. My father had a special whistle for us, but since I can't whistle I used to carry a small whistle around my neck so I could let my kids know where I was. Now I do the same with my grandchildren.
- Teach her never to walk off with a stranger.
- Make sure your grandchild can recognize her surroundings when she's close to home by pointing out landmarks on every trip: "There's the mailbox on the corner, and there's the blue gate, and our house is the next one."

Outings with young children

Special days out don't have to cost a lot of money. If you're able to take one grandchild at a time you'll find that they are so happy with the extra attention, they'll enjoy the simplest of activities. And whether it is a walk in the country or a day at the beach, be prepared to make endless stops to look at anything that catches his attention. You have the luxury of time, so enjoy it.

Plan carefully

When planning an outing, always try to consider what your grandchild's personality can cope with best. If he's a quiet child who has a long concentration span, you can take him anywhere, from a museum to a garden center, and point out the things around him. If, on the other hand, he's very active, he'll need more space to run around in and a trip to a playground might be more appropriate.

Days out together
It's wonderful taking a walk and having a picnic in the country or trip to the beach. Most grandchildren think it is even more special if Grandpa comes along too.

Always take enough liquids and snacks to keep your grandchild happy for the full duration of the trip. Don't take a trip of any kind if you or he is feeling unwell; the day is bound to be a disaster, so don't feel guilty about postponing an outing to another time.

If traveling by car with your grandchildren, keep in mind that safety regulations are much stricter now than when our children were young, so make sure you are up to date with the latest requirements. If you are likely to be

driving your grandchildren often, you might want to invest in your own car seats or booster seats, depending on their ages. If it is just an occasional trip, you can borrow seats from your children. Make sure seats are correctly installed and used. Most children get restless after an hour or so of driving, so make regular stops so they can run around and get rid of excess energy.

"If traveling by car with your grandchildren, keep in mind that safety regulations are stricter now, so make sure you are up to date with the latest requirements"

Car safety

Always check the latest updates on car safety regulations for children, but here are few reminders for you:

- Never travel in a car holding a baby or child on your lap, or try to put a seat belt around you and a child.
- A child should always travel in a child seat and restraint that is appropriate for his weight and size.
- Rear-facing seats are safest for babies and can be used in the front or rear seats of the car.
- Rear-facing seats should not be used in the front of a car with a passenger airbag.
- Never buy used car seats or safety restraints. They could have been damaged in an accident.

Your trip checklist

As with any kind of outing with your grandchildren, the essential thing is to plan and prepare well in advance. The following tips will all help to make things go more smoothly for you:

- Try to travel early in the morning or at night, when the traffic is quiet.
- Carry a large bag of spare clothes for your grandchild, be philosophical about accidents, and change him quickly into dry clothes.
- For safety, tape cutlery to the inside of food containers.
- Take some soft clothing like a fleece or sweater that your grandchild can use as a pillow. A rug is useful too.
- Have a supply of bags into which cartons, bottles, and wrappers can be put after use.
- Take a box of baby wipes to clean dirty hands and faces, and some tissues.
- Have a blind to block out direct sun.
- Some favorite CDs can be a godsend. Stories are good, as are songs you can sing along to together.

Indoor play

You can do your grandchild no greater favor than to play games at all times, even when you don't feel like it. Never turn down the request "Grandma, will you play with me?" Every time you get down on the floor and play with your grandchild you're giving her lessons that help her grow and develop.

The best games require thinking and that's very good for her developing brain, which increases in size by *three times* in her first 12 months. Every situation you find yourself in lends itself to playing and learning—learning all kinds of skills by using her body and mind according to the games you play. As an experienced grandma you will make up your own, but here are a few ideas for fun and games:

"The best games require thinking and that's very good for your grandchild's developing brain which increases in size by three times in her first 12 months"

Down on the floor
Your grandchild will be thrilled if you get down on the floor with her and play. From newborn until she can sit up, she'll love these games.
- Sit on the floor next to her, make eye contact, hold your gaze, talk, and laugh.
- Rock her body gently back and forth.
- Let her grasp your fingers and slowly pull her up a few inches.
- Clap her hands together.
- Clap her feet together.
- Wiggle her legs and arms.

Sitting upright on your knee
Hold your grandchild on your knee as you play games. The closeness will help her feel safe and loved.
- "Read" books and magazines together—let her crumple the pages of magazines and listen to the sound.
- Play clapping songs to foster talking; try "Patty-Cake, Patty-Cake."
- Put a burp cloth over her head and play Peek-a-Boo.
- Hold her wrists and pull her to standing for strong legs and good balance.
- Shake rattles and noisy toys together.
- Play "Round and Round the Garden" to awaken hands and fingers for holding, gripping, and letting go.
- Play "This Little Piggy Went to Market" to prepare feet and toes for standing, balancing, and walking.

Bath time games

What my grandchildren love best is when I get in the bath with them.
Try the following ideas for bath time fun:

- Pouring from one container to another
- Pouring from large to small (too much) and small to large (too little),
  to teach about volumes
- Blowing bubbles
- Hair washing games—make hair spikes with shampoo lather
- "Swimming" underwater—getting her face wet to prepare for swimming.

Gentle games on the changing mat

A learning game
Peek-a-Boo has
important lessons for a
baby, for example, that
even when she can't
see something it still
exists. It also helps her
learn to anticipate
what comes next and
wait for it to happen.

Even diaper changing time is a chance for games. Maintain eye contact with
your grandchild all the time as you play. Babies love the following games:

- Turning over to reach a toy—have a special array of favorite changing
  mat toys on hand and keep talking about them while you change your
  grandchild's diaper.
- Baby gym—hold hands and pull her upper body off the mat.
- Hold her feet and lift her lower body off the mat.
- Baby massage as you apply moisturizing cream.

Early ball play for hand-eye coordination

Start ball play as soon as your grandchild can sit unaided and swivel her trunk to reach behind her. Here are some ways to help:

- Roll a large, soft beach ball toward her so it rolls between her legs, and say "catch."
- Ask her to send it back to you and say "catch" when you grasp it.
- Then say "ready, set, go" to prepare her and roll it toward her.
- As she gets older, roll ever smaller balls toward her and encourage her to toss them back.
- Take a soft ball and bounce it off your head a few times—she'll laugh.
- Then gently bounce the ball of her head—hopefully she'll laugh again.

Never stop reading

I read stories to my grandchildren at any available opportunity. For instance, if I'm taking them to school and we're early, I sit down and start reading a book to them. In no time, all the other children have gathered around!

- Use any spare moment to read to your grandchild.
- Remember that it's never too early to start reading to your grandchild.
- Start with soft cloth books.
- Read floating books in the bath.
- Put soft books in her crib and later on in her bed so she can sleep with her favorites.
- Read bedtime stories every chance you get, out of bed or curled up in bed with your grandchild.
- Buy books for your grandchild or get them from the library—try to take a new book each time you visit your grandchild.

One-on-one time
Once children have siblings, they love to have some one-on-one time with Grandma or Grandpa. You can concentrate on activities that they like best and really boost their self-confidence.

- Give books as presents—then read one and say why you bought it.
- Buy for your grandchild books you loved as a child and say why you liked them so much.

Helping your grandchild to play happily with other children

If your grandchild doesn't want to join in games with other children at a party or gathering, you can be a safe haven. Never try to force her to take part. Let her sit on your knee or stay close to you until she feels ready to join the group.

- Take some of her toys and play with them together—encourage other children to join in.
- Watch the others with her and say, "That looks like fun. Shall we go and join them?"
- Read a story aloud to all the children with your grandchild sitting safely on your knee.
- Get down on the floor with all the children and play with all their toys. Talk about what you're doing.
- Be fair about sharing, for example:
  - one minute each with the toy
  - your turn, her turn, my turn
  - say the word "sharing" over and over
  - act out sharing and say "Look, Grandma is sharing the doll with you and Daisy"
  - "Will you give me one of your raisins? Thank you! Good girl!"
  - "Sara's playing with the sand, shall we play in the kitchen and make a cup of tea for your doll?"

Answer questions
Children are always curious and love to know how things work. As a grandparent, you'll have the patience to answer their endless questions and explain all kinds of concepts.

Learning and playing in the kitchen

The kitchen is a great place to spend time with your grandchildren, and there are so many ways in which she can have fun while learning.

- Let your grandchild sit next to you while you prepare food and explain what you're doing and why.
- Sink play—wrap your grandchild in an apron or dish towel and provide lots of utensils. Then stand her safely on a chair and play water games.
- Invite your grandchild to cook with you—adding ingredients to the mixture, putting vegetables into the pan, holding a container for you.
- Let her make what my grandchildren call "stuffs"—they all love mixing the most unlikely ingredients together into a big bowl to make a potion; this is a great way of exercising their creativity.
- Ask her to mop up a mess with a paper towel.
- Let her wipe low surfaces with a damp cloth to clean up and be helpful.
- Wash paintbrushes in the sink to make rainbow water.

Let her help cook
Encouraging a child to help in the kitchen has benefits for everyone. You're teaching her about cooking and being independent. And when she's old enough she can cook a meal for you!

Outdoor play

Playing outside with your grandchild can be strenuous and you may find yourself using muscles that haven't been worked for some time. Getting and keeping fit will make outdoor play a lot more fun and save your aches and pains. It takes stamina, so it may be worth putting in some time in the gym.

In the park

I find a visit to the park with my grandchildren both thrilling and, to be honest, tiring. I have to admit that trying to keep my eye on all three at once can be testing, and occasionally I've panicked when one has disappeared from sight. But we all have such a good time and there's so much space that I've taught myself to be watchful and vigilant, and I have become more agile and strong than I ever thought I could be.

Climbing

Most parks have magnificent climbing apparatus designed to help children of all ages graduate to more and more difficult ascents and descents. Children can test their strength and determination for themselves but I'm not averse to giving the occasional leg up in a testing situation, or saying, "Never move a hand or a foot until you have all four firmly in place."

> **" *Going to the park with my grandchildren has made me more agile and strong than I ever thought I could be* "**

Sliding and swinging

At the top of the jungle gyms there are slides to aid descent, some of them dizzyingly high, but if your grandchildren are like mine that won't stop them. They'll test themselves by coming down on their tummies, head first. Reassure yourself that they won't be afraid of heights when they're older, and just be there to scoop them up at the bottom.

From the time they can sit up, babies and children love swings, and parks have them for all ages. You'll probably have to push your grandchildren until your arms, shoulders, and back ache, but you'll be in prime position for keeping an eye on their safety.

Kicking, throwing, and catching

A back yard may be big enough for simple throwing, catching, and kicking games but outside in the park these games come into their own. Your grandchild can watch big children playing soccer, frisbee, and tennis and want to join in and play. In the park mistakes don't matter, and as long as you're prepared to retrieve the ball you'll all have fun. Get your grandchild a baseball mitt when he's about six, to make catching a piece of cake.

Pointing out nature

Whenever you're outside with your grandchild you can point out some aspects of nature:

"Leaves drop in the fall."

"It must be winter because…? There are no leaves on the trees."

"We know it's spring because the snowdrops/daffodils/crocuses are out."

"When the birds sing early in the morning it's called the dawn chorus."

"When a racoon comes into our yard it's searching for food."

"A child's sense of achievement can be built nowhere as effectively as in a swimming pool, where tiny increments of skills are mastered"

At the swimming pool

Even if you don't swim yourself, visits to a pool are not to be missed. First, it's family fun all together. Second, you'll see your grandchild being brave, adventurous, trying hard, and achieving great physical feats. Third, if you do swim you can pass on a few tips. Learning to swim is an essential life skill so you're doing your grandchildren a big favor if you help to get them used to water, be happy in it, and make some effort to move around in it. A child's sense of achievement can be built very effectively in a swimming pool, where even tiny increments of skills are mastered.

Safety is the prime concern. Keep home pools covered or fenced when not in use. Inflatable clothing should be worn at all times until a child can swim three yards without help. Goggles are good eye protection in public pools where chlorine concentrations in the water are high.

A vital skill
Not only is swimming a delight in itself but it is also a vital safety skill, so the sooner your grandchild learns to swim the better. Go along to the pool with her and do yourself some good too.

Cycling

I've bought my grandchildren wooden pedal-less bikes that they can propel with their feet at the age of two. They learn so much from them (balance, steering, judgment of speed, how to brake and stop, safety on the street) and it develops total body strength. These bikes are good preparation for real bicycles, and it's an easy graduation from one to the other—ignoring training wheels.

Other ideas for outdoor fun with your grandchildren

Sand pit

All children love playing with sand and it's a fun way to learn about building sand castles, making homes for plastic animals, and pressing out different shapes.

Trampoline

All my grandchildren have loved a baby version from the age of 18 months and it's great for developing strength for the whole body as well as teaching coordination and balance. All you have to do is applaud.

Playhouse

There's no better place to act out adult roles, and if you squash yourself in and have an imaginary tea party or, better still, bring some sandwiches and cupcakes, you'll be every grandchild's favorite.

Gardening

Even showing your grandchild the rudiments is teaching them about how things grow, and with a little pot of strawberry plants they can follow the flowers turning into edible fruit. Quite an achievement.

Watering

Teaching your grandchild that all plants need water to grow is a good lesson to learn. Bring a toy watering can, towel, and fork with you to encourage him to take care of plants.

Feeding the birds

A simple bird table and a string bag of nuts tied to a bush remind children that wild animals need caring for, and it's exciting to watch birds come to feed. A bird book will help your grandchild start to recognize species and you can have fun watching out for them together.

Vacations with your grandchildren

Taking your grandchildren away on vacation alone or with your partner is an ambitious project. You'll remember the glitches that used to occur when you traveled with your own young family and how to resolve them. But much has changed since then. It helps to check everything out and plan meticulously.

One at a time

I most enjoy taking just one grandchild at a time. That way each one gets my full attention and we spend lots of time just one on one, making the vacation really bonding and special. I've found this one-on-one time especially soothing for a grandchild who's feeling dethroned by the arrival of a new baby. In one fell swoop you can restore the child's confidence, sense of security, and self-belief, and of course you'll make a friend for life.

A vital skill
Be ready to help your grandchild when you're doing things together outdoors. He'll still get a great sense of achievement by tackling something he couldn't manage by himself.

A golden rule is to make sure that your hotel has facilities for children, and that the staff really likes children. Check it out as much as you can and look at reviews on the internet. Things to look for in a hotel include such child facilities as a day-care center, a place where you can take your grandchild for an early dinner, a children's menu, high chairs and cribs, a playroom, and an outdoor play area that's properly supervised. It's worth going to some trouble to ensure at least some of these things are available, because if your grandchildren aren't happy, you won't enjoy the vacation yourself.

What to pack

Use the following checklist to make sure you've got everything you need for your grandchild. If you're traveling by plane, get to the airport early, so you don't have to rush your grandchild, and give yourself plenty of time to get there.

- Passports and inoculation documents, if necessary
- The baby bag
- Stroller
- A thermos for cool drinks
- Favorite toys, games, books, and CDs
- Sun hat
- Swimwear and flotation items
- Plenty of changes of clothes
- Sting cream
- Water resistant sunscreen
- Lotion for sunburn
- Insect repellant cream
- Children's antihistamine medicine
- Children's acetaminophin or ibruprofen
- Something to suck on during take-off and landing.

Sun safety

Children don't have very much skin pigment, so they have less protection than adults from the sun's ultraviolet rays. Being exposed to direct sunlight can lead to skin damage and skin cancer later in life. To protect your grandchild:

- Use sunscreen of at least SPF 30 for toddlers and SPF 50 for babies, in addition to the natural protection of clothes and shade. Twenty minutes before going out, apply the lotion to the face, neck, ears, and the back of hands and feet. If she's running in and out of the water or swimming pool, reapply sunscreen every half an hour or so.
- In very hot weather, avoid taking her out in the sun between 11 am and 4 pm.
- Dress her in a wide-brimmed hat and protective clothing.
- Be aware that she's still at risk on cloudy days.
- Make sure the stroller has a protective hood or umbrella to shade her.
- Dress your child in a sun hat and UV-resistant clothes and apply sunscreen regularly when she's outside playing in the sun.

Grandparenting from a distance

Not all of us are lucky enough to live around the corner from our grandchildren. You may be in another city, or a different country entirely, and see your family only once or twice a year. But it's still possible to keep in touch, and the latest technology makes this easier than ever before.

Get online

When your grandchildren are tiny you'll be eager to know every detail of their development, and if you're not living nearby you'll be dependent on the parents to provide regular updates. If you don't already have access to a computer and the internet it's a good idea to get online now, since this will make keeping in touch with you much simpler for them.

Parents can email photos regularly so you can see pictures almost immediately rather than waiting for prints to arrive. And many new parents set up a social networking page on the internet when their baby is born so they can put up pictures and bulletins regularly for all the family to look at, wherever they are. This can be a great way of keeping everyone up to date with the baby's progress without too much effort.

Moms and dads can also capture key milestones on video and send them via the internet so Grandma and Grandpa can share the thrill of their grandchild's first smiles and steps. And you could record yourself reading stories so your baby grandchild starts to get to know your voice.

> **"** *If you live far away from your grandchildren, the internet makes it so much easier to keep in touch* **"**

Initiate contact

As your grandchildren grow up, don't always wait for them to get in touch with you. It's just as important—if not more so—for them to hear from you, and there are lots of ways to do that. Simplest of all is to pick up the phone and give your grandchild a call, so do this often once he's old enough. Don't just speak to him after talking with his parents; call him separately. That way he'll feel special. Don't worry if young grandchildren don't say much. Just hearing your voice is good and you'll probably be told that he was smiling as he listened to you.

Better still, call your grandchildren via the internet, using an internet telephone system—that way you can see them, too, and this makes such a difference if you can't be together very often. Being able to see each other makes talking to the younger ones easier and they can hold up their drawings or new toys for you to admire. What's more, many of these systems are free, so you can talk as long as you like without worrying about bills.

We're all into email and texting these days and both are great ways of keeping in constant touch with older grandchildren. If you don't already use email, it's certainly worth mastering it, but don't forget the old-fashioned mail. All children love getting cards and packages in the mail and they don't have to contain expensive presents—just little things such as a package of fun stickers or some colored pencils. Encourage them to send you little pictures and cards, too, by giving them some stamped addressed envelopes.

Whenever you can, make the effort to travel to your grandchildren. All the technology in the world can't replace the feeling of holding your grandchild in your arms.

Calling home
It's great to talk to your grandchild via the internet. When she comes to stay with you, you can keep in touch with Mom and Dad that way too, so she doesn't get homesick.

"I'm worried I'm going to lose my grandchildren"

Sue's son and daughter-in-law are splitting up and she's terribly upset. She's also frightened about whether she'll still see her grandchildren, a girl of six and a boy of four. She says her world revolves around them and she dreads losing touch. Her daughter-in-law is talking about joining her own parents in Australia and starting a new life. Sue doesn't feel she could afford to visit and thinks that her daughter-in-law isn't taking her feelings into account. What can she do?

happen. I think Sue's best option for the moment is to forget all that self-pity and start thinking how she can protect her grandchildren from the trauma of their parents' separation.

Many children of divorced parents say that their grandparents were a source of great comfort while their parents were splitting up. So in Sue's place I'd be making myself available to the grandchildren as a shoulder to cry on and someone who can banish their fears by answering their questions and reassuring them.

I'd advise Sue to think about how she can protect and comfort her grandchildren at this time. And if they do move away, there are so many ways she can keep in touch

It's very sad that Sue's son's marriage is breaking up and that will be traumatic for her, but even worse for her grandchildren. Perhaps Sue should focus on them and the difficulties ahead, not on herself?

When parents divorce, grandparents can be the rock whom children can turn to and be sure of love and security. It would be a shame for Sue if her daughter-in-law moved to Australia because she'd have to make more effort to play that important role in her grandchildren's lives, but it may never

The children will have sensed long ago that Mom and Dad weren't getting along. I suggest Sue takes every chance to be around them because she can help ease their passage into the next phase of their lives, whether it's at home or in Australia.

If they do move away, there's no reason for Sue to lose contact with her grandchildren. She can stay in touch through letters, cards, phone calls, texts, emails, and internet calls. And she could start saving up now for a first visit.

9 Grandparent as Caregiver

Grandparents today are vital carergivers in many families, whether for a few hours of babysitting or in a larger role of regular care.

Occasional caregiving

Most grandparents will look forward to taking an active role in looking after their grandchildren, whether it's a few hours of childminding and babysitting, or being a more important part of their grandchild's care on a regular basis.

In one way, being an occasional caregiver of your grandchild would seem the best possible option for grandparents—you have as much contact with your grandchild as you like, but you can escape whenever you want. I've found the most useful frame of mind in which to approach being a caregiver is to downgrade your self-importance and see yourself simply as a helper.

Morning cuddle
Sleeping at your son or daughter's house after baby-sitting can be the most restful option, and you'll be rewarded with a cuddle from your grandchild in the morning.

Daytime care

Doing some babysitting for grandchildren up to school age is invaluable for your own children. And you'll feel doubly rewarded—for the favor you're doing them and for the chance to spend some time on your own with your grandchild.

Having a framework into which you fit your care means that the time you spend with your grandchild becomes very precious because it's limited. Your care time is finite. What you do may be limited by where you do your babysitting. It's one thing to be a visitor in your grandchildren's home for a morning or an afternoon; it's another to do the babysitting in your own home. It's different because the rules are different.

In your children's home you will feel constrained, quite rightly, by the way they prefer to do things. I think the only way to go is to conform to their rules, unless you're given a free hand. This may require changing your own priorities on occasion and swallowing your pride.

" Babysitting gives you the chance to spend time alone with your grandchild and get to know her "

A successful role as a grandparent means putting yourself last. Your views only count if solicited. Ego has no value in grandparenting. You have a longer perspective—you're sensitive to the needs of others and your ego has evolved. Put that on display and compromise if necessary.

Your home or theirs?

Here are some things to think about and discuss with your family when deciding whether to do any babysitting in your home or your children's. I find I naturally behave differently in each place. In their house I see myself as a just a babysitter, not as someone who wants do do things her way.

- **Housekeeping** In your own home you might cut corners once in a while, but in your children's home—hardly ever.
- **Timetables** In your own home you can be flexible. In your children's home, stick to the routines.
- **Initiative** In your own home you can use your own, but in your children's home, conform to house rules.
- **Decisions** In your own home, do what you think best. In your children's home, do what they think best.
- **Emergencies** In your own home, use your judgment in an emergency. In your children's home, confer with your child.

- **Feeding** In your own home you can take a relaxed approach. In your children's home, go by the rules.
- **Discipline** In you own home you can be flexible. In your children's home, stick to the guidelines.

Babysitting at night

Your son and daughter will enjoy their evening out much more when they know you, who love and care for the children as much as they do, are at home with them. In this instance, it's your experienced and respected supervision

"Your son and daughter will enjoy their evening out much more when they know that you, who love the children as much as they do, are caring for them"

that's needed, and even though you'll be left in charge you're really standing in for your grandchild's parents. You're a surrogate parent and your children will not expect you to stray too much from what they would usually do in the evening. If you're asked to babysit late, it's a good idea to have your trip home planned, whether it's a lift home from your son or daughter, or a taxi.

Sleeping over

To make the evening as comfortable as possible, you might opt to sleep over so you can go to bed before your children get home from their night out, rather than waiting up for them.

This is really a good option for all concerned and one of my favorites: your grandchild gets you at bedtime for stories, songs, and lights out—possibly even baths, if your stamina is up to it. She can enjoy your relaxed approach to bedtimes, then once she's in bed, you get some me-time.

It's a good idea to have agreed on a couch or bed where you're going to sleep. I started out sleeping on the couch, but as I got older I've decided I needed a real bed and my children understand this. One of things I love best about sleeping over is when a warm little body snuggles in next to me in my bed in the morning and we snooze together.

If you do sleepovers with any regularity, it's good to have your overnight bag stashed away somewhere so you don't have to carry very much with you.

Breakfast treat
All children love mixing, so when you make a breakfast treat, such as pancakes, let your grandchild help stir the batter. She'll enjoy eating them even more.

Decide with your children who will get up for the grandchildren. If you're feeling generous you can take on breakfast duties when the grandchildren wake. My three granddaughters in one of my families are up at the crack of dawn so we all go down to the kitchen and make pancakes as a weekend treat. Another benefit of sleeping over on the weekend is that I can take them to their gymnastics class—and enjoy lots of grandma pride watching them!

A bigger role

Some grandparents might want to take on a larger, and more regular, role in their grandchildren's care, perhaps involving a couple of whole days a week or more. This is quite a big undertaking and, in my experience, it's better to make an agreement right at the start between you and your son or daughter about just what your care will encompass.

This may seem too formal for some grandmas, but I know from the mail I get that trouble will ensue if your expectations and those of your son or daughter don't match, especially when the subject is the well-being of a grandchild who's so close to you and whom you feel so emotional about.

I'd always advise you think through what you'd like to do and what you wouldn't; what you can do and what you can't; how much of your time you can commit and how strenuous your activities will be. It's wise to mull over all these points with your partner and come to an agreement. Then you can get down to the nitty-gritty, weigh the practicalities and the implications.

Granpa's role
Even if Grandma does most of the caregiving, get Grandpa involved in the fun too.

The importance of grandparent care

You should know that grandparents are vital caregivers for young families in the US. It is estimated that 40 percent of grandparents, who have grandchildren under age 13 and live within an hour from them, are currently providing child care for their grandchildren while parents are at work or school. Another 19 percent have done so in the past. In total, nearly 60 percent of grandparents are either providing child care for their grandchildren or have in the past.

Your house or theirs?

The answer to this question may seem obvious, but it isn't always. Below are a few things to weigh and consider while you and your son or daughter are deciding what might be best. Think about yourself as well as your children. For example, their house might have lots of stairs, so taking care of your grandchild there might be tiring for you if you are used to living at one level in an apartment or house.

- **Equipment** All your grandchild's equipment—stroller, high chair, crib, and so on—is at your children's home so it's convenient, or would you be willing to fix up a room in your house as a nursery?
- **Familiar surroundings** Your grandchild is most comfortable in his own home and may get fretful, even with you, if he's in less familiar surroundings, such as your house.
- **Kitchen** Their kitchen will be safe for babies and young children. Yours might not be, so you might need to make some changes.
- **Storage** Do you have room to store the various equipment needed for your grandchild, such as a stroller and high chair?
- **Yard** Their yard is probably safe and equipped for children, perhaps with a sand box or play area. What about yours? Do you have any poisonous plants, for example?

" Being paid or not paid is a conversation you should have before you take on substantial care of your grandchild "

Should you be paid?

There may be some very straightforward guidelines that will help you to decide what you think is fair. If, for instance, you'll be giving up time when you could earn money, then it would seem reasonable to be paid for your child care. The same would apply if you have to give up paid work to help your son or daughter out with child care.

Whatever your situation, whether or not to be paid is a conversation you should have before you take on substantial child care, if only to prevent it from becoming a point of contention later. The kind of things you could think about are:

- Do you think it's fair that you get paid? (Ordinarily you would earn money in the time you give to child care, so why not?)

- Do you think it's fair to be paid per half day or by the hour?
- And if so, how much for each?
- Would it be easier all round if you agreed a "price for the job," that is, for all the child care in a week on a regular basis?
- Find a benchmark—do you know other grandmas who do child care? Ask what payment they get. Look at grandparenting websites for guidance.

What you might do

My advice is always to see yourself as a mother's helper, but how far does that extend? Will you be seen as a cleaning lady, a laundress, and a cook too? The answers really depend not only on how much you want to do but on how strong you are. You may have a lot of stamina at 60, but your strength might well have ebbed away by 65 or so. So within these constraints I think you could prepare yourself by making a couple of lists along these lines:

Jobs I'd love to do which wouldn't be too tiring
- Making meals
- Going to the park
- Changing and dressing the baby
- The occasional trip to the store for something really needed.

Jobs I wouldn't mind doing occasionally
- Putting laundry in the washer and dryer
- Folding the laundry and putting it away
- Filling and emptying the dishwasher.

Jobs I wouldn't want to do
- Cleaning
- Putting away all the toys at the end of the day
- Mopping the kitchen floor
- Changing bed linens.

Then, ask your child what, besides your list, they would like to suggest. Make sure you agree everything well in advance so that you don't feel put upon or that you're being asked to do more than you can do. It's fine to say what you can and can't manage.

Shared approaches

If you're going to be taking on a lot of caregiving for your grandchild, then I feel it's only fair that you have a say in how he's cared for. This is especially relevant if you care for him in your own home. So I think there has to be a degree of give and take between you and your daughter or son. All of you have to know from the start is where your freedom begins and ends, and to feel comfortable about how you're going to do things. You'll be familiar with many routines, but some of the areas you might want to talk about are:

- What is the **format** of meals—for example, vegetables first, then meat/fish/protein and fruit for dessert?
- What sort of "**treats**" does your son or daughter permit —fruit smoothies, yogurt, raisins?
- What may your grandchild drink—water, diluted fruit juice, milk?
- Are **naptimes** exact?
- How should you deal with **tantrums**?
- Should you use a **time out**?

Ongoing conversations

It's never good to let irritations fester so why not agree that you and your daughter or son will have regular dialogue and feedback sessions? This sets up a mechanism to voice your happiness with the arrangement and to air grievances. I say regular, but I don't mean planned. Your feedback can come from a natural occurrence: "You know, today I noticed she really enjoyed it when I sat her on the bench next to me as I made her lunch—is that OK with you?"

Home safety

You'll remember all the safety basics from your own days as a parent and will automatically watch out for your grandchildren. But, particularly when you have your first grandchild, your own home might not be as safe for children as it should be, and there will be things you need to keep in mind if young grandchildren are going to be spending time with you.

Many everyday household items are dangerous to children. Every year a large number of children are brought to the hospital because they have fallen from windows, burned themselves on stoves or been scalded by hot drinks, choked on small objects, or swallowed household chemicals. Your grandchild is naturally adventurous and inquisitive, and it is too easy to underestimate the dangers she faces as she explores her environment, especially in the light of her developing mobility and manipulative abilities.

Safety equipment

Your home should be protected with **smoke alarms** on each level. These alarms are inexpensive and easy to install. They must be attached to the ceiling, not a wall, to be totally effective.

The kitchen is the most likely place for a fire to start, so you should keep **fire extinguishers** there. They need to be checked regularly for pressure, and may need to be replaced annually.

Make sure that **windows** remain firmly closed, or have locks so they can be opened only a little bit, especially on upper floors. Avoid placing furniture under windows—children will be tempted to climb up and risk falling.

Don't forget
You probably already have smoke alarms in your house, but make sure they are working. And if your home has stairs, you'll need to install stair gates.

Install a **stair gate** at the top or bottom of the stairs. The bars should be vertical so that your grandchild can't climb on them, and the gate should have a childproof lock.

"Your grandchild is naturally adventurous and inquisitive, and it's too easy to underestimate the dangers she faces as she explores her environment"

Fire safety

House fires can be fatal if you or your grandchild inhale smoke and toxic fumes. Fortunately, there are lots of ways in which you can minimize the likelihood of a fire and lessen the damage that it can do.

- Don't smoke indoors—or at all around your grandchild.
- Don't leave pots or pans containing hot fat unattended.
- Keep flammable liquids locked away.
- Use fireguards on any open or gas fire.
- Store matches and lighters out of your grandchild's reach.
- Buy fire-resistant furniture.
- Make sure your grandchild's clothing is fire-resistant—check the labels.
- Replace fire extinguishers every year.
- Keep a dry powder extinguisher and a fire blanket in the kitchen.
- Install smoke alarms, and check regularly that the batteries are working.
- Install a carbon monoxide detector, available from home improvement stores.
- If you light candles in your home, keep them well out of the reach of children and pets. Never leave a lit candle unattended.
- Make sure you know what to do if there's a fire; for example, smother a pan fire with a fire blanket, damp cloth, or pan lid.

Watch out
If you're going to be taking care of your grandchild in your home, install childproof locks to cabinets, and store medicines well out of reach.

General safety tips

If this is your first grandchild, you'll probably be a bit out of practice with the precautions listed here. Check out your house with the following in mind and try to spot any potential problems, then deal with them.

- Store all medicines in a locked cabinet or on a high shelf—even if they have childproof caps.
- Keep disinfectants, cleaning fluids, and so on in their original containers and put them out of children's reach.
- Store sharp objects such as knives and scissors out of reach.
- Don't use tablecloths. A toddler can so easily pull them and everything on them on to her head.
- Don't leave hot beverages or glasses of alcohol where a child could reach them.
- Don't leave cigarettes, matches, or lighters lying around.
- Keep bowls of pet food out of reach of children.
- Watch out for trailing cords from lights, TV, and stereo equipment.
- Watch out for blind cords, and hook them up out of reach.
- Use outlet covers to stop your grandchild from poking objects into electrical outlets. Neutral-colored are best, so they don't attract your grandchild's attention.
- If you have a wood, gas, or electric fire, always use a hearth safety grate or screen.
- Don't keep poisonous houseplants such as irises or daffodils.
- Make sure any fragile, breakable items are kept out of your grandchild's reach.
- Store plastic bags out of your grandchild's reach.
- Make sure there are no potentially dangerous items, such as electric shavers or curling irons, within a child's reach. Something that is an everyday item to you can be lethal for a child.
- Your pets might not have had much contact with young children before. Never leave your grandchild alone with pets, particularly dogs, unsupervised. Once children are old enough, teach them how to behave safely with animals.

"I just can't do as much any more"

Elaine is 74 and the primary caregiver for her three grandchildren, since their mom and dad (her son) both work. They have a nice house and car, and go away on vacations. Elaine says they are very generous to her and always have been. They pay her really well and they all get along. Her problem is that her strength is failing her and she doesn't have the energy that she used to. She gets so tired and by the end of the day she just wants to fall into bed. How can she tell them she can't do as much any more?

and insisting that nothing is too much trouble. How would they know anything is wrong? It's time for Elaine to be honest.

Fortunately, Elaine has such a good relationship with her family that she can have a very constructive conversation about her concerns. I'd suggest that she explains that she's worried about her health. Elaine might also point out that if she became sick, she might not be able to help them at all, so she'd like to cut back. They'll probably be shocked not to have figured out that she's less strong than she was and will be

I'd urge Elaine to explain to her children that she's worried about her health and needs to do less. I'm sure they will understand and be very kind and thoughtful

I know how tempting it is to just press on and drag yourself around until you're exhausted. But health is too important, and if Elaine goes on like this she could make herself really sick.

Elaine's children are good people. They obviously love her and want to take care of her too. They've shown their consideration for her for a long time and they probably don't realize just how tired she's getting, taking care of the three grandchildren. She just keeps going, putting on a brave face,

really kind and thoughtful. I found myself in a similar position and my children were wonderful when I explained I had to do less. I'm sure Elaine's will be too.

Some might say that Elaine's children should have noticed that her strength was failing, but these days parents are so busy and stressed they expend all their energy on keeping the family going. And even if they had noticed, they might have found it difficult to handle. It's better that Elaine takes the initiative and tells them the truth.

10 *First Aid*

You'll remember what to do for minor childhood illnesses, but it is a good idea to brush up on your first aid techniques, just in case of an emergency.

Emergency first aid

As a grandparent you'll inevitably have to deal with a few minor accidents and cuts and bruises when taking care of your grandchildren. You may also be faced with more major emergencies, so it's good to be prepared.

My emergency

Just to underline the importance of this, I had my own emergency recently. One of my little granddaughters, two-year-old Evie, was having a sleepover with me. I so enjoy having her and we'd had a lovely evening. Much to my horror, she woke me in the middle of the night in a terrible state, unable to breathe. She had a very bad attack of croup. And I panicked! I rushed around the house, thinking: "What should I do? I'll never forgive myself if anything

"If you're worried about a child, get help and fast. An emergency medical technician (EMT) told me that they would always rather be safe than sorry"

happens to that child." I even considered grabbing a kitchen knife and performing an emergency tracheotomy! Fortunately, common sense prevailed and I stopped and thought about what I've said in all my books: if a child is having trouble breathing, call an ambulance. I did. They came with admirable speed, took us to the hospital, and all was well.

So don't hesitate. If you're worried about a child, get help and fast. The EMT who came to us that night told me that they would always rather be safe than sorry where children are concerned.

Home first aid kit

Keep these items in a clearly marked box with an airtight lid. Make sure you know how to use each one properly. You may also like to keep some infant acetaminophen for treating pain or fever in young children.

Crepe bandages	Surgical tape	Scissors
Open-weave bandages	Antiseptic wipes	Thermometer
Triangular bandage	Calamine lotion	Tweezers
Gauze dressings	Band-aids	Safety pins
Wound dressings	Shaped band-aids	Cotton balls

Priorities

If your grandchild has an accident it's important to get your priorities right. Ask another adult to get help while you go through the questions listed here. Detailed instructions are given on pages 202–5.

If there's no one else around, work through the list of questions and if necessary, give chest compressions and rescue breaths (CPR) to the child for two minutes (five rounds) before calling for emergency help.

Is there any danger?

Make the area safe. Don't put yourself at risk —don't approach your grandchild if doing so puts you in danger. If it's safe to do so, remove the danger from the child.

Is your grandchild conscious?

Keep calling her name clearly and loudly. Tap her foot or her shoulders. (*Never* shake her to see if she is conscious.)

If she responds, she is conscious. Don't move her. Check her carefully and treat any injuries.

If there is no response, she is unconscious. Check to see if she is breathing.

Is she breathing?

Open your grandchild's airway by tilting her head back and lifting her chin. Lean close to her mouth to listen for breathing and feel it against your cheek. Look along her chest to see if it is rising and falling. Check for no more than 10 seconds.

If there are no signs of normal breathing, begin CPR (see pages 202–5). Continue until help arrives.

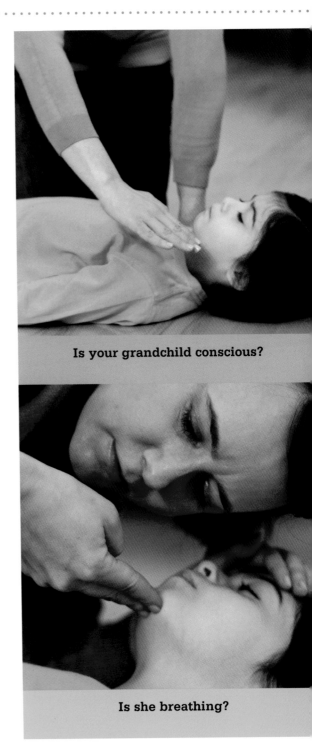

Is your grandchild conscious?

Is she breathing?

The CAB *of resuscitation*

In an emergency, if your grandchild loses consciousness, go through the following key points in the order given:

C is for Chest Compressions

Start CPR with 30 chest compressions followed by 2 rescue breaths (see pages 202–5).

A is for Airway

This must be open and clear. To open it, tilt the child's head and lift the chin. (see pages 202 and 204).

B is for Breathing/Ventilation

If the child shows no signs of breathing, remove any obstruction from the mouth, but never sweep the back of the throat.

Changing advice

First-aid advice is constantly reviewed and improved and may well have changed since your time as a parent. Refreshing your knowledge will help you deal with accidents quickly, effectively, and calmly. To give first aid effectively you need to understand and practice the techniques detailed on the following pages. Make sure you have a first-aid kit that's accessible in an emergency, but stored out of your grandchild's reach. You might want to have another first-aid kit in the car, particularly if you often drive your grandchildren around.

"First-aid advice is constantly reviewed and improved and may well have changed since your time as a parent, so it's worth refreshing your knowledge"

First-aid training

In order to make use of the following emergency procedures you need to learn them by heart. If you have to spend time referring to this book in order to refresh your memory, precious time will be lost and the delay could be the difference between the life and death of a child.

This book can't make you certified. To learn first aid properly you need to complete a course of instruction and pass a supervised examination. The American Red Cross (redcross.org) offers first aid courses suitable for parents and grandparents.

Unconsciousness

If a child has lost consciousness and isn't breathing, her heart will stop and she's at risk of brain damage. You need to make a fast assessment of her condition in order to know what first-aid treatment to give.

Priorities

If a child is unconscious, the muscles that keep the tongue off the back of the throat don't work. So the tongue falls back and blocks the air passages. If the child is unconscious, the first priority is to open the airway by tilting her head back, then check her breathing (this is the first question the EMT will ask).

If she is breathing, place her in the recovery position (see below) to keep the airways open and clear, then call for help. If she's not breathing, give cardiopulmonary resuscitation (CPR—see pages 203 and 205). If you're by yourself, give CPR for one minute before you call the ambulance.

To place a baby in the recovery position, cradle her in your arms with her face slightly toward you and her head lower than her body in order to keep the airway open (see below).

To place a child in the recovery position, kneel beside her and place the arm closest to you at a right angle to the body with the elbow bent. Bring the other arm across her chest, toward you, and place the back of her hand against the cheek closest you. Grasp the thigh that is farthest away from you and pull the knee up, keeping the foot flat on the ground and placing it next to the closer knee. The uppermost leg then acts as a "prop." Roll the child over into a resting position with her knee bent and her head resting on her hand (see below).

ecovery position for baby

Recovery position for child

Unconscious infant (under one year)

An unconscious baby who is not breathing needs to be given cardiopulmonary resuscitation (CPR)—chest compressions and rescue breaths—in order to get air into her lungs. First of all make the following checks.

Check for response

To check whether a baby is unconscious, tap the sole of her foot and call her name. If there is no response within about 10 seconds, she is unconscious. Yell for help.

Open the airway

Make sure the baby is on her back on a firm surface or on the floor. Put one hand on the baby's forehead and carefully tilt her head back. Then lift the chin with your fingertips. This lifts the tongue away from the back of the throat. Don't press against the soft tissues under the chin since this can block the airway.

Check for breathing

Look, listen, and feel for signs of breathing. Look along the baby's chest and abdomen and look for movement. Listen closely for sounds of breathing and feel for breaths on your cheek. Do this for no more than 10 seconds. If the infant is not breathing, begin CPR (see page 203).

If the infant is breathing, hold her in the recovery position (see page 201) until help arrives. Hold the infant in your arms with her head tilted downward so she doesn't choke on her tongue or inhale vomit.

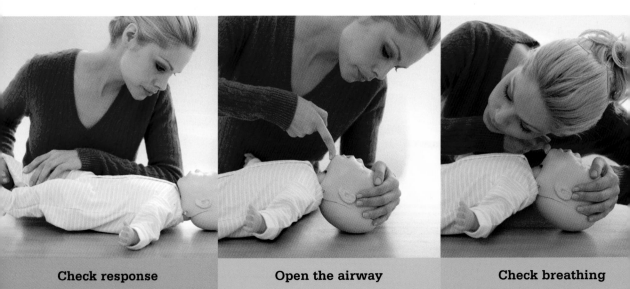

Check response   **Open the airway**   **Check breathing**

How to give CPR for babies under one year

Prepare for chest compressions
Place the tips of your first two fingers onto the center of the baby's chest. Don't press on the ribs, the lower tip of the breastbone, or the soft part of the upper abdomen.

Give chest compressions
Press down sharply on the chest with the tips of the fingers. Release the pressure and allow the chest to come back up, but don't remove your fingers from the chest. Repeat to give 30 compressions at a rate of 100 per minute.

Check airway
Lift the chin with one fingertip and keep the other hand on the forehead. Pick out any obvious obstructions from the mouth but do not poke a finger down the baby's throat.

Give two initial rescue breaths
Take a breath, put your lips over the baby's nostrils and mouth, making a complete seal. Breathe gently into her mouth and nose until you see her chest rise (about one second). Remove your lips and let the chest fall (one second). Give two rescue breaths at a rate of one every three seconds.

Repeat compressions and rescue breaths
Repeat compressions and rescue breaths for five cycles—approximately two minutes—then call for an ambulance if this has not already been done. Keep giving CPR until the ambulance arrives or the baby starts to breathe normally.

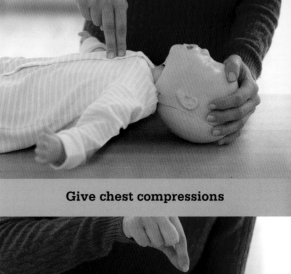

Give chest compressions

Check the airway

Give rescue breaths

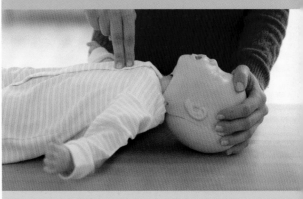

Repeat chest compressions

Unconscious child (one year to puberty)

An unconscious child who is not breathing needs to be given cardiopulmonary resuscitation (CPR)—chest compressions and rescue breaths—in order to get air into his lungs. This is possible because there is enough oxygen in your exhaled breath to keep another person alive. The chest compressions "pump" the oxygenated blood around the body.

Check for response

To find out if the child is conscious, tap his shoulder and keep calling his name. If he doesn't respond, he's unconscious. Yell for help.

Open the airway

Make sure the child is lying on his back on a firm surface or on the floor. Put one hand on his forehead and carefully tilt his head back. Lift his chin with the fingertips of your other hand. Don't press the soft tissues under the chin since this can block the airway.

Check breathing

Look, listen, and feel for signs of breathing. Look along the child's chest and abdomen for movements. Listen for sounds of breathing and feel for his breath on your cheek. Do this for no more than 10 seconds. If he is not breathing begin chest compressions.

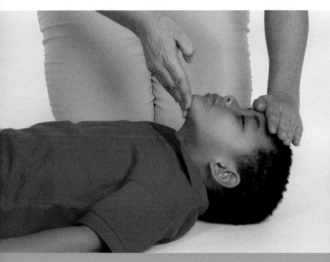

Open the airway

Check breathing

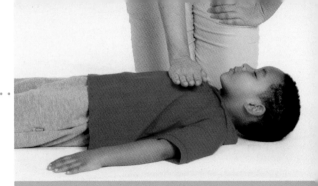

CPR *for children*

Prepare for chest compressions
Put the heel of one hand on the center of the child's chest. Be careful not to press on his ribs, the lower tip of the breastbone, or the soft part of the upper abdomen.

Give chest compressions
Press down sharply on the chest with your hand, depressing the chest by about one-third of its depth. Release and allow the chest to come back up completely, but don't remove your hand. Repeat to give 30 compressions at a rate of 100 per minute. Allow about the same time for compression and release.

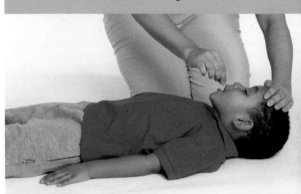

Give chest compressions

Check airway
Lift the chin with two fingers and keep the other hand on the forehead. Pick out any obvious obstructions but do not poke a finger down the child's throat or sweep the mouth.

Give two initial rescue breaths
Using your finger and thumb, pinch the child's nostrils closed. Take a breath, put your mouth over his, making a seal, and breathe out until his chest rises (one second). Remove your lips and let the chest fall (one second). Give two breaths at a rate of one every three seconds.

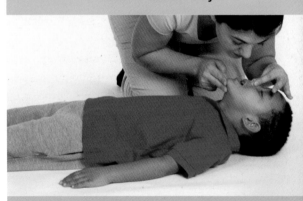

Check the airway

Repeat compressions and rescue breaths
Repeat compressions and rescue breaths for five cycles—approximately two minutes—and call for an ambulance if this has not already been done. Keep giving CPR until the ambulance arrives or the child starts to breathe normally.

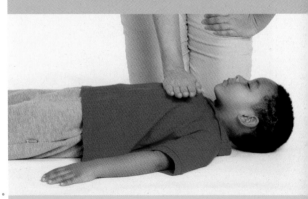

Give rescue breaths

Repeat chest compressions

Other emergencies

Other potentially serious situations that might arise when you're taking care of grandchildren include choking, burns and scalds, head injuries, drowning, and electrical shock. You might also have to deal with poisoning if your grandchild swallows something she shouldn't, so it's good to be prepared.

Choking

Children are very prone to choking since they often put small things in their mouths. They may also choke on food. You need to act quickly, since if the airway becomes completely blocked or a child is unable to get sufficient oxygen into the lungs, she may lose consciousness. If the airway is partially blocked, she will be able to cry, speak, or cough, and breathe. If the airway is completely blocked, she will be unable to speak, cough, or breathe and needs urgent assistance.

Helping a choking baby
Lay the baby along your arm and give back slaps with the heel of your hand. If this doesn't work, turn her onto her back and try chest thrusts.

For a baby (under one year)

If a baby chokes on food or a small object, she will quickly become distressed and you need to act fast to clear the obstruction. Follow the steps below to clear the obstruction.

1. Give back slaps

Lay the baby face down along your forearm, with her head low, and support her head and shoulders. Give up to five blows with the heel of your hand between the shoulder blades.

2. Check the mouth

Turn the baby face up and check her mouth. If you can see the obstruction, hook it out with your finger. Don't put your finger down her throat or try to sweep the mouth since this may push the object farther in.

3. Give chest thrusts

If back slaps don't work, hold the baby on her back and place two fingers on the lower half of her breastbone, just below the nipple line. Push five times, inward and upward toward the head. Check the mouth again.

4. Repeat

If the chest thrusts don't work, repeat steps 1–3 three times, then call an ambulance.

For a child (one year to puberty)

If the child is old enough to understand what you are saying you can reassure her and encourage her to try to cough up the obstruction before you begin treatment. If the child loses consciousness at any stage, be prepared to begin CPR (see pages 204–5).

Encourage coughing

If the child is breathing, reassure her and encourage her to cough up the obstruction.

Give abdominal thrusts

Try abdominal thrusts. Put your arms around the child's upper abdomen. Place your fist between the navel and bottom of the breastbone and grasp it with your other hand. Pull inward and upward sharply and repeat up to five times.

Start CPR

Start CPR if the victim becomes unresponsive (do not perform a pulse check). After 30 chest compressions, open the airway. If you see a foreign body, remove it but do not perform blind finger sweeps or put your finger down her throat because this may push obstructing objects farther in. Attempt to give two breaths and continue with cycles of chest compressions and rescue breaths until the object is expelled. Call an ambulance and continue the chest compressions and rescue breaths until help arrives.

Encourage the child to cough   **Give abdominal thrusts**

Burns and scalds

If your grandchild's clothing catches fire, get her to immediately lie down on the ground and smother the flames with a heavy wool coat or blanket (never use anything made of nylon, since it will catch fire). Seek medical help for any burn on a child. Either call a doctor or ambulance, or go to the hospital.

What to do

- Hold the burn under cold running water for 10 minutes—use a hose or shower for a larger burn. Do not apply lotions, fat, cooling sprays, or gels.
- Unless clothes are sticking to the burned area, gently remove them—cut them off if necessary. Do not remove anything stuck to the skin.
- Cover burn with plastic wrap or a clean plastic bag. Place it lengthwise over the burn, not around it since tissues may swell. If you don't have these, use a sterile dressing. Never use "fluffy," linty-cloth, or adhesive dressings.
- Do not touch the area or attempt to burst any blisters.
- Seek medical advice. If the child loses consciousness, check breathing and call an ambulance. Be ready to begin CPR (see pages 202–5).
- If the burn is major, call an ambulance, then lay her down and pour water over the affected area for 10 minutes or until the ambulance arrives. Check that she is breathing. You may need to treat her for shock (see page 211). If she loses consciousness be prepared to resuscitate her (see pages 202–5).

Treating a burn
For a minor burn, hold under cool running water for 10 minutes or so. For a larger-area burn, use a shower or a hose. Seek medical help for any burn on a child.

Poisoning

As you know, young children are often tempted to swallow things they shouldn't. Here's what to do if you suspect your grandchild has eaten or drank something poisonous:

What to do

- Try to get her to tell you what she has swallowed and how much. If she is unable to tell you, look for evidence such as open or empty bottles, or nearby poisonous plants or berries.
- Call Poison Control (1-800-222-1222) and tell them what your grandchild has swallowed. Keep the poison to take to the hospital if advised.
- Never attempt to make her vomit, since this may cause further harm.

Bleeding

Small cuts and scrapes are very common in children of all ages, but it is important to be able to recognize more serious wounds, and know how to treat them to prevent significant loss of blood.

What to do

- Press the wound firmly to reduce bleeding. Help your grandchild lie down and raise the injured area above the level of his heart.
- Cover the wound with a sterile dressing and bandage.
- Call an ambulance or go to the hospital if the wound will not stop bleeding after 10 minutes, if it is very deep or gaping, or if there is dirt or any foreign object lodged in the wound.

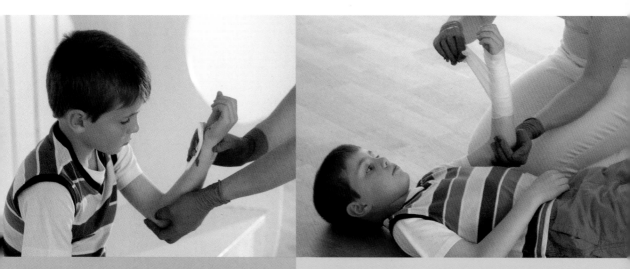

1 Raise the cut and apply pressure | **2 Cover with a sterile dressing and bandage**

Head injuries

If your grandchild bangs his head he will normally recover within minutes. If he bangs his head fairly hard he may have some temporary swelling. Head injuries that should cause concern are those that cause severe bleeding or concussion— where the brain is shaken inside the skull causing temporary unconsciousness. Another more serious condition called compression can develop hours or days later if a blow to the head causes swelling around the brain—look out for drowsiness, headaches, and nausea after a head injury.

What to do

- If your grandchild is dazed, help him sit or lie down on the floor. Don't sit him in a chair, because he may fall off. Give him a cold compress to place against the bump to reduce the swelling.
- If your grandchild loses consciousness, check his breathing and call an ambulance.

"Head injuries that should cause concern are those that cause severe bleeding, concussion, or compression"

- Keep monitoring his breathing while he is unconscious and be prepared to begin CPR (see pages 202–5) if necessary.
- If he loses consciousness briefly, then recovers, he may be concussed —look out for dizziness, nausea, headache, and memory loss. Get medical help. Monitor his level of response (for example, alert or dazed) for the next few hours and note any changes. Don't leave him alone.
- If he stays conscious, monitor him closely for 2 hours. If he is drowsy, stunned, or dazed, or suffers from recurrent nausea or vomiting, he may be suffering from bleeding inside the brain (compression). This is an emergency and he needs to go to hospital. If there is bleeding from the scalp, press a clean pad firmly to the area to stop the flow. If the wound is long or jagged, take him to the hospital. Do not touch the wound with your fingers. If the cut is small, clean it with soap and water and put a dressing on it.
- Watery blood leaking from the ears or the nose may indicate a skull fracture. This must be treated as an emergency. Don't plug the ear; let any discharge drain away.

Drowning

Babies and young children can drown quickly in even a few inches of water. Never leave your grandchild unattended in the bath, and follow these steps if she gets into difficulties:

What to do
- Lift her out of the water and carry her with her head lower than her chest, to reduce the risk of inhaling water.
- Remove any wet clothing and cover her with a dry towel to keep warm.
- If she is unconscious and breathing, put her in the recovery position and call an ambulance. If she is not breathing, begin CPR (see pages 202–5).

Electrical shock

Minimize the risk of electrical shock by installing covers on outlets and keeping electrical appliances well away from young children. If your grandchild does get an electrical shock, here's what to do:

What to do
- Turn the power off at the circut breaker.
- If you cannot turn it off, stand on an insulating material such as a book or wood box and use a piece of wood, such as a broom handle, to knock the source of electricity away from your grandchild.
- Alternatively, wrap a dry towel around your grandchild's feet and use this to pull her away from the source of the shock.
- If she is unconscious, call an amblance. If she is not breathing, begin CPR (see pages 202–5).

Shock

Severe injuries such as a large burn or serious bleeding can cause your grandchild to go into shock. Symptoms are: pale, sweaty skin that is cold to the touch; a rapid, weak pulse; shallow, fast breathing.

What to do
- Help her lie down on a blanket and cover her with another blanket for warmth. Check for any injuries, such as bleeding, and treat them as best you can (see page 209).
- Call an ambulance.
- Carefully raise her legs and support them on cushions or a pile of books, so that they are above the level of her heart.

Bites and stings

Your grandchild probably loves the company of animals but, particularly if he gets overly excited and is not as gentle as he should be, bites can happen. Bites and stings from insects and other creatures are not usually serious, unless there is an allergic reaction, but can be extremely itchy.

Animal bites

Animal bites can happen if your grandchild is teasing or playing boisterously with a domestic pet. Although being bitten can be traumatic, bites are not usually serious. The main danger is that, if the animal bites deeply, bacteria will be lodged in the wound, making it vulnerable to infection.

The first thing you should do is reassure her, since she will probably be fairly frightened. If she was bitten because she was teasing the animal you should explain this to her and emphasize that it is an isolated incident.

" *Being bitten can be traumatic for a child but not usually serious. The first thing to do is to reassure your grandchild* "

What to do
- Wash the wound thoroughly with warm water and cover with a dressing.
- If the bite is severe, try to control bleeding with direct pressure and raise the wounded part of the body.
- Cover the wound with a dressing held in place with a bandage and take your grandchild to hospital. She may need a tetanus injection if her immunizations are not up to date.
- If your grandchild is bitten by a dog while you are traveling seek medical treatment at once, since rabies injections may be needed.

Snake bites

There are a variety of venomous snakes in the US including coral snakes, water moccasins, copperheads, and rattlesnakes. Other countries have other venomous creatures. Depending on the snake, symptoms of a bite can include puncture marks in the skin, pain, redness, and swelling around the bite. In very severe cases, there may be impaired breathing, sweating, vomiting, and impaired vision.

What to do

- Keep your grandchild calm. Help him to lie down with head and shoulders raised. Call an ambulance.
- While waiting for help, keep him still and try to prevent the venom from spreading. Apply a pressure bandage at the site of the bite. Then apply another pressure bandage from the bite to as far up the limb as possible.
- Mark the site of the bite if you can and make a note of the snake's appearance to help doctors choose the correct antivenom.

Insect bites and stings

The pain of most insect bites and stings fades within hours. Stings in the mouth or throat, however, are serious, because the swelling can obstruct the airway.

What to do

- If the stinger is visible, brush or scrape it off with the edge of credit card. Do not use tweezers, which could squeeze more poison into the wound.
- Raise the affected area if possible and apply a cold compress.
- For a sting in the mouth, give him an ice cube to suck (if over one year old) or some cold water to sip. If swelling develops, seek emergency help.
- For jellyfish stings, pour lots of vinegar over the area to incapacitate the stinging cells. If you don't have vinegar, pour plenty of seawater over it.
- If she experiences swelling of the face and neck, puffy eyes, red blotchy skin, or wheezing and gasping, your grandchild may be having an allergic reaction and you should call for emergency help.

For bites: Once the wound is clean, cover it with a dressing, held in place with a bandage.

For stings: Raise the affected area and apply a cold compress, such as an ice pack, to minimize swelling.

If you can see the stinger protruding from the skin, gently brush it off with the edge of a credit card

Bumps and scrapes

You'll remember all too well how to deal with minor cuts, bruises, and other mishaps, but it's useful to refresh your knowledge and be up to date with the latest advice. Most of the time these accidents are not serious and you can treat your grandchild at home with comfort and simple first-aid techniques.

Cuts and scrapes

As long as a cut is superficial and is not infected (this is a risk with cuts by fingernails, plants, or animals), it should not require treatment. A scrape is simply an abrasion of the skin that leaves the surface raw and tender. A cut that bleeds profusely can lead to shock (see page 211) so treat it as an emergency. A very jagged cut may require stitches, and with a deep or dirty cut there is a risk of tetanus (see page 209 for treating serious wounds).

What to do

- Rinse the wound under running water and pat it dry with gauze. Cover it with sterile gauze.
- If possible, raise the injured part above heart level and support it there to slow the flow of blood. Do not touch the wound.
- Clean the area around the wound with soap and water. Wipe away from the wound and use a clean piece of gauze for each wipe. Pat dry. Remove the gauze and apply a sterile dressing.
- If the cut is bleeding profusely or if it is dirty or deep, take the child to the hospital.

Blisters

When the skin is burned or subjected to pressure or friction a blister may form as a protective cushion. They are common on the heels of the feet if a child's shoes don't fit correctly or if she wears shoes without socks. Blisters are rarely serious unless they are the result of bad sunburn, they burst and become infected, or they are very large and painful, in which case consult a doctor.

Do not burst a blister. In a day or two new skin will form underneath, the tissue fluid will be reabsorbed, and the blistered skin will dry and peel off.

What to do

- Wash the area with clean water and gently pat it dry with a sterile pad. If you can't wash the area, keep it as clean as possible.
- Cover the blister with a dressing larger than the blister. Blister band-aids are best since they have cushioned pads, which give extra protection.

Bruises

Active children often get bruises from falls and bumps, and they are rarely serious; they usually take 10–14 days to disappear completely.

What to do

- Minor bruises need no treatment, just a hug if your grandchild is upset.
- Consult a doctor immediately if pain from a bruise gets worse after 24 hours (this could indicate a fracture) or if your grandchild repeatedly has bruises with no apparent cause (this could indicate a serious condition).

Splinters

Unless splinters are embedded in the flesh or they prove too painful to remove, they can be dealt with very easily at home.

What to do

- Find out what kind of splinter it is—glass fragments must be removed by a doctor.
- If the splinter is not glass, draw it out at the same angle it entered using a pair of tweezers sterilized over a flame. Make sure it does not break.
- Clean the skin with soap and water.
- If the splinter is completely embedded in your grandchild's skin, or the wound is dirty, it may need attention from a doctor.

Removing a splinter
Sterilize your tweezers over a flame and let them cool. Gently pull the protruding end of the splinter out at the same angle it entered. Then clean the area with soap and water.

Feeling unwell

You'll remember the signs of illness in a young child—he might be pale, listless, and refuse food—but if you're worried, call your doctor. To help your doctor, observe all you can about your grandchild's symptoms; the more information you can give, the better the chance of an accurate diagnosis.

Temperature

Just in case your grandchild has a fever when you are taking care of him, it's good to refresh your memory on taking temperatures. Today's thermometers are much easier to use than those I had when my children were young.

Normal temperature

A baby's normal body temperature ranges between 97° F (36° C) and 100.4 °F (38° C). If a baby under 3 months has a temperature of 100.4 °F or higher, you should call the doctor. Hypothermia develops if his temperature falls below 95° F (35° C). A child's body temperature varies according to how active he has been, and with the time of day, so if he does have a fever, take his temperature again after 20 minutes—it might have been only temporary. Never judge whether or not a child is sick on temperature alone. He can be very ill without a high temperature or quite healthy with one.

Thermometers

I used to have a mercury thermometer, but these can be dangerous if they break. Digital thermometers are widely available, and if you are going to be taking care of your grandchild at your own house, it's important to get one.

What to do

The rectal method is best for young babies, especially under 3 months of age. It is not difficult to do and is much more accurate in a baby. Otherwise, oral, underarm, or ear thermometers are fine.

For an armpit thermometer, raise your grandchild's right arm. Put the thermometer in his bare armpit, lower his arm over it, and hold the arm down until you hear a "beep." To take his temperature orally, ask your grandchild to open his mouth, then place the thermometer under his tongue. Ask him to close his lips—but not his teeth—over the thermometer so that the seal is airtight. Make sure he's not gripping the thermometer with his teeth. Leave it in his mouth until you hear a "beep." Remove it and read the number in the window.

For an ear thermometer, place the tip inside the ear until you hear a beep—it will take about 1 second. It is easy to use, even while your grandchild is asleep.

Vomiting

Single incidents of vomiting may simply be the stomach's reaction to unfamiliar or too much food, but you should consult a doctor if your grandchild vomits repeatedly over a six-hour period, or if the vomiting is accompanied by other symptoms such as diarrhea, a fever, stomach pain, or headache.

What to do

- Reassure her and give her a cloth to wipe her face. Put a bucket by her bed in case she needs to vomit again.
- Give her small amounts of water to drink every 10–15 minutes, to prevent her from becoming dehydrated.
- When the vomiting is over, help her brush her teeth to take the taste away.

Meningitis

Meningitis is a serious illness, and it is important to be aware of the symptoms, since your grandchild will need emergency treatment if the disease is confirmed. Seek medical advice immediately if you suspect your grandchild has meningitis.

Symptoms

- High fever (as high as 102.2°F (30°C)); stiff neck and headache
- Lethargy, drowsiness, and confusion; inability to tolerate bright light
- Purple-red rash that does not fade when you press a glass against it
- Bulging fontanelle in babies younger than 18 months
- Cold hands and feet; mottled or pale skin
- Joint and limb pain.

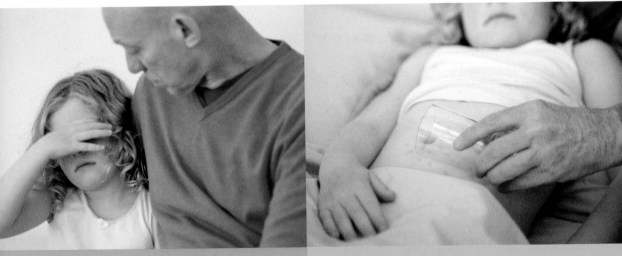

Is she sensitive to light?   **Check the rash by pressing a glass against it**

Index

Useful addresses

Grandparenting groups

GRAND

A website for advice, health and wellness, family money, and other grandparent-related information

Website: www.grandmagazine.com

Grandparents.com

A website for information on activities, babysitting, travel, and education

Website: www.grandparents.com

Grandparents Rights Organization

A nonprofit founded to educate and support grandparents and grandchildren and to advocate their desire to continue a relationship that may be threatened.

Website: www.grandparentsrights.org

General childcare advice

American Academy of Pediatrics

www.aap.org http://www.aap.org

Child Care Aware

Information and support for working parents
Tel: (800) 424-2246
Website: www.childcareaware.org

Child Care Bureau

Information about child-care tax credits and child-care financial assistance
Website: www.acf.dhhs.gov/programs/ccb

Families and Work Institute

Publishes numerous handbooks
Tel: (212) 465-2044
Website: www.familiesandwork.org

National Child Care Information Center

A national clearinghouse linking parents to online child care
Website: www.nccic.acf.hhs.gov

The Women's Bureau

US Department of Labor
Offers free work and family resource kit
Tel: (800) 827-5335
Website: www.dol.gov/wb

Zero to Three

Resources related to child care
Tel: (202) 638-1144
Website: www.zerotothree.org/site/PageServer

Caring for twins and more

The National Organization of Mothers of Twins Clubs

Support and information for families of twins, triplets, and more
Tel: (248) 231-4480
Website: www.nomotc.org

The Triplet Connection

National clearinghouse for education, referrals, and support
Tel: (435) 851-1105
Website: www.thetripletconnection.org

First-aid and accidents

American Red Cross

The American Red Cross helps prepare communities for emergencies and keep people safe every day
website: www.redcross.org/

National Center for Injury Prevention and Control

Information about injuries and coping with a traumatic event
Tel: (776) 488-1506
Website: www.cdc.gov/ncipc

Poison Control

Tel: 1-800-222-1222

Safe Kids

Information on preventing childhood injury
Tel: (202) 662-0600
Website: www.safekids.org

SIDS Alliance

Information on SIDS prevention and support for families after the death of a baby
Tel: (800) 221-7437
Website: www.sidsalliance.org

Acknowledgments

Most of all, I'm indebted to Jinny Johnson, whose editing skills have helped to steer me through the vicissitudes of bringing this book together in a way that we both wanted, in order to serve today's grandparents.

The photographs in this book thrill me and so my grateful thanks to photographer Ruth Jenkinson and art director Isabel de Cordova.

The editorial team at Dorling Kindersley, particularly Daniel Mills, has given me unswerving support – many thanks to them all. And of course I must thank my assistant Hajni Domokos for typing up the original manuscript.

And last but not least, thank you to my four sons and their wives for allowing me to be the granny I always imagined I would be, and to my grandchildren who lovingly help me to live the role of being their granny.

DK would like to thank:
Creative publishing manager: Anna Davidson
Medical consultant: Aviva Schein
Proofreader: Salima Hirani
Indexer: Susan Bosanko
Photographer: Ruth Jenkinson

The publisher would like to thank the following for their kind permission to reproduce their photographs:

(Key: a-above; b-below/bottom; c-center; f-far; l-left; r-right; t-top)
Alamy Images: Vadim Ponomarenko 94; Loisjoy Thurstun / Bubbles Photolibrary 121. **Corbis:** Arthur Baensch 157; A. Chederros / Onoky 67; Kevin Dodge 141bl; Jose Luis Pelaez, Inc. 179; LWA-Dann Tardif 18; Ocean 140br; Anthony Redpath 181; Tim Hale Photography 21; Mike Watson / Moodboard 189; Larry Williams 48. **Getty Images:** The Agency Collection / Moodboard 113; The Agency Collection / PhotoConcepts 49; The Agency Collection / Rubberball Productions 176; Elie Bernager 129br; bilderlounge / Alessandro Ventura 166br; Blend Images / John Lund / Annabelle Breakey 147; Botanica / Rachel Weill 76; Brand X Pictures / Jupiterimages 170bl; Comstock Images / Thinkstock Images 92; Cultura / Colin Hawkins 127; Cultura / Fiona Jackson-Downes and Dirk Lindner 159; Cultura / Frank and Helena 152br; Cultura / Henglein and Steets 178; Cultura / i love images 38; Digital Vision / Andersen Ross 100; Iconica / Jerome Tisne 185; Iconica / Jose Luis Pelaez 72, 73; Iconica / Tom Grill 71; Image Source 86; The Image Bank / Chris Stein 142; The Image Bank / Dan Bigelow 155tr; The Image Bank / Henrik Sorensen 170br; The Image Bank / LWA 97; Johner Images / Nyman, Fredrik 173; Luc / STOCK4B 118; OJO Images / Tom Merton 105; Photodisc / Mel Yates 140bl; Photodisc / Reggie Casagrande 22, 25; Photographer's Choice / Clarissa Leahy 137; Photographer's Choice / Fraser Hall 108; Photographer's Choice / James Ross 166bl; Photographer's Choice RF / Dana Hoff 193bl; Purestock 119; Riser / Camille Tokerud 14br; Stock Image / Cultura / yellowdog 15br, 39; Stockbyte / SW Productions 145; Stone / Barbara Maurer 35, 126; Taxi / Alistair Berg 141br; Taxi / Jean-Noel Reichel 155cr; Taxi / LWA 102; Taxi / Yellow Dog Productions 154; Taxi Japan / ULTRA.F 174; Tetra Images 45; UpperCut Images / John Fedele 104; Workbook Stock / OJO Images / Justin Pumfrey 180. Photolibrary: Asia Images RM / Alex Mares-Manton 195; Creasource 155br; F1 Online / Jean Glueck 171bl; Imagebroker.net / Ulrich Niehoff 192bl; Justin Paget 63; Stockbroker / Monkey Business Images Ltd 13.

Jacket images: *Front:* **Alamy Images:** Andrew Paterson fcra (boots). **Getty Images:** Photographer's Choice / Peter Dazeley ftr; Stone / Siri Stafford crb (baby). **iStockphoto.com:** Michael Fernahl ftl (teddy); Michelle Junior bl (child's toy). *Back:* **Getty Images:** Stone / Siri Stafford c. **iStockphoto.com:** Michael Fernahl cl.

All other images © Dorling Kindersley
For further information see: www.dkimages.com